Marriages of

CHATHAM COUNTY,

NORTH CAROLINA

1772-1868

Compiled by

BRENT H. HOLCOMB

CLEARFIELD

Reprinted for
Clearfield Company, Inc., by
Genealogical Publishing Co., Inc.
Baltimore, Maryland
2006

INTRODUCTION

This volume contains abstracts of all extant marriage bonds issued in Chatham County, North Carolina, from 1772-1868, when marriage bonds were discontinued. The abstracts of the bonds were made from a microfilm copy of the bonds and are arranged in alphabetical order by the name of the groom, each entry further providing the name of the bride, the date of the bond, and the names of the bondsmen. To facilitate research, brides and bondsmen are also listed in the index. Additionally, abstracts of the entries in the marriage register, 1851-1868, are included as well. The original marriage register remains in the office of the Register of Deeds, Chatham County Court House, Pittsboro, North Carolina. My thanks to the Register of Deeds for permission to include those marriages in this publication. The marriages in the register were recorded in the order in which they were turned in by the officiant. Some were recorded several years after the marriage took place. The names of the grooms and brides from the register are included in the index. From the scant number of bonds and the large number of entries in the register, it is obvious that many marriage bonds are missing from this county.

The reader should keep in mind that the name of the groom on the bond is spelled as the name was signed, or in the case of a person who could not write, the way it was signed for him. The name of the bride appears as it was spelled by the clerk or the person making out the bond. Since the bride did not sign, the spellings may vary widely from the way the name would properly be spelled.

Marriage bonds are the only public records of marriage prior to 1851. Although the marriage bond law was enacted in 1741 and remained in force until 1868, the clerk of the county court was required only from 1851 to keep a register of all marriages performed by license (issued with the bond).

The researcher should bear in mind that bonds alone are not proof that a marriage took place, only that a marriage was intended. The entries in the register are proof the the couple was married. Also, not everyone who married in Chatham County between 1772 and 1868 is identified in this work, for some marriages were performed after publication of banns and no bond, license, or other public record of marriage was required.

BRENT HOWARD HOLCOMB, C. G.
Columbia, South Carolina

CHATHAM COUNTY NC MARRIAGES 1772-1868

Abanathy, Clayton & Elizabeth Walden, 15 Dec 1841; Smith Abanathy, bm.

Abbott, John & Maria Edwards, 14 June 18--; James Brown, bm.

Adcock, Henry & Elizabeth Riddle, 5 Dec 1831; John S. Guthrie, bm.

Aldredge, Samuel & Polly Headin, 7 Sept 1821, H. D. Bridges, bm.

Allen, Cratis & Mary Hatwood, 28 June 1851; Alfred Hatwood, bm.

Allen, Joseph & Polly Conselman, 25 July 1832; George Baggs, bm.

Alston, Joseph J. & Decimus Palmer, 4 Dec 1839; Henry Goodwin, bm.

Alston, Joseph J. Jr. & Pamelia De Graffinreidt, 20 Dec 1836; John H. Hawkins, bm.

Andrew, John & Elizabeth Whitehead, 18 Oct 1828; William Whitehead, bm.

Andrew, William & Rachael Hadley, 10 Jan 1840; James McBane, bm.

Argo, Hemmons, & Milly Roe, 21 Dec 1816; Solomon Roe, bm.

Atwater, Jahaza & Sarah Stone, 12 Nov 1833; John S. Stroud, bm.

Atwater, Wesley & Julia Horton, 6 Dec 1841; Jehiel Atwater, bm.

Bagley, James & _____, __ Feb 1813; Abram Petty, bm.

Bails, Solomon & Mary Moore, 28 March 1812; John Gilbert, bm.

Baldwin, Joseph & Julia Burnitt, 27 March 1833; Atlas J. Baldwin, bm.

Barker, Bishop & Elizabeth Pounds, 30 Jan 1816; Benjamin Wells, bm.

Barbour, Burrell & Elizabeth Armstead, 17 June 1839; Hillery H. Yeargin, bm.

Barber, John Q. & Nancy Armstead, 18 March 1839; Thomas Whitehead, bm.

Barber, Moses & Hannah Edwards, 3 Jan 1835; William Jordan, bm.

Barham, Thomas & _____, 25 Feb 1808; Peter Farrar, bm.

Beal, Asa & Chloe Morand, 28 Nov 1817; William Thompson Jr., bm.

Beal, Elisha & Lydia Barber, 3 June 1840; Asa Beal, bm.

Beck, Samuel & Catharine Kirk, 14 March 1818; David Beck, bm.

Bell, James & Lydia Chapman, 25 Apr 1814; William Clark, bm.

Bland, John & Elizabeth Hatch, 20 May 1841; William Clark, bm.

Bland, Oliver & Catharine Williams, 20 Aug 1833; John Neal, John Gunter, bm.

Bland, William & Elizabeth McBain, 2 Jan 1813; Thomas Bland, bm.

Boling, Tapley & Sally Ellington, 16 Jan 1838; William Bryant, bm.

Boling, Taply & Drucilla White, 10 Feb 1817; William Pyland, bm.

Boon, Thomas W. & Sindarilla Seagroves, 24 May 1833; James M. Stedman, bm.

Boyd, Archibald & Phebe McPherson, 6 May 1829; William Boyd, bm.

Boyd, John & Mary Bright, 23 May 1810; William Moody, bm.

Bradley, William & Rachael Farmer, 10 July 1779; James Moon, bm.

Brady, Nelson & Margaret Johnson, 10 Dec 1839; William S. Edwards, bm.

Brafford, Robert & _____, 23 Dec 1852; Allen Brewer, bm.

Brake, Wesley & Catharine Wicker, 4 Apr 1833; William T. Horne, bm.

Branson, Levi & Lovy Williams, 5 March 1831; David Pickett, bm.

Brantly, Brooks & Sally H. Brooks, 15 Apr 1812; William Ragland, bm.

Bray, Calvin & Harriet Avent, 26 Feb 1842; Luther Clegg, bm.

Bray, Harris & _____, 15 Sept 1819; William Bray, bm.

Bray, Henry & Issabell Edwards, 29 Jan 1811; Nathan Edwards, bm; Henry Bray, son of James Bray, wit.

Bray, Joab H. & Emily J. Brooks, 18 Oct 1853; Jer. D. Bray, bm; m 18 Oct 1853 by Gera Lane.

Bray, John & Susannah Hadley, 21 March 1817; Jeremiah Brewer, bm.

Brewer, Jeremiah & Ann Bray, 11 Sept 1817; John Bray Junr., bm.

Brewer, John & Keziah Johnson, 5 Sept 1817; Edward Teague, bm.

Brewer, Samuel & Muied(?) Trip, (no date, during admn. of Gov. David L. Swain); James Tropling, bm.

Bridges, Horace D. & Martha Gee, 21 Oct 1812; Nicholas P. Smith, bm.

Bridges, William & Sally Justice, 28 Sept 1816; Horace D. Bridges, bm.

Bright, Charles T. & Levina Fields, 29 March 1833; Thomas Thompson, bm.

Brooks, Edward W. & Sarah Brooks, 18 March 1840; Timothy T. Brooks, bm.

Brooks, Richard & Nancy Self, 16 July 1809; Willis Jones, bm.

Brooks, Samuel & Caly Bright, 8 March 1817; Benjamin Gunter Junr., bm.

Brooks, Terrell & Susanah Warren, 2 April 1792; John Dabney, bm.

Brooks, Terrell & Nancy Harris, 2 Dec 1827; Josiah Headen, bm.

Brown, Daniel & Patsy Bray, 23 Dec 1818; Mark Bray, bm.

Brown, James & Susannah Higdon, 18 Nov 1812; Thomas Gordon, bm.

Brown, Jepthra & Sarah Pilkinton, 12 Dec 1833; John Brewer, bm.

Brozus, William & Rebecca Wamack, 24 Dec 1815; William Ausly, bm.

Bryan, Daniel R. & Susan Clark, 7 Jan 1840; Wesley Hanks, bm.

Bryant, William & Nancy Wilson, 14 May 1852; m 16 May 1852 by M. Thrailhill, J. P.

Buchannon, Joseph & Martha Buchannon, 19 Dec 1822; Henry Claiborn, bm.

Buchhannan, Lemuel & Mary Ledbetter, 19 Sept 1838; Fred Rollins, bm.

Burgiss, William W. & Elizabeth Lewis, 8 Oct 1836; James Barker, bm.

Burke, John R. & Nelly Womack, 12 Feb 1839; H. H. Burke, bm.

Burns, Alvis & Henrietta Burns, 23 Oct 1839; Jackson J. Gilmore, bm.

Burns, George W. & Frances Tysor, 22 Nov 1841; John W. Stedman, bm.

Burns, John Junr. & Mary Brantley, 30 Jan 1792; William Brantly, bm.

Burns, Thomas & Lavinia Burns, 21 Sept 1841; George W. Stedman, bm.

Burroughs, Bryant & Maria Gilbert, 30 Dec 1839; John Harman, bm.

Burrow, Benjamin & Betsey Allred, 20 July 1833; Paris Pearce, bm.

Bynum, Corney & Margaret Clegg, 7 Jan 1834; Turner Bynum, bm.

Bynum, Mark Jr. & Mary Clegg, 27 Feb 1839; Turner Bynum, bm.

Bynum, Turner & Julia C. Ward, 20 Nov 1833; Joseph Bynum, bm.

Campbell, Daniel & Betsey Emerson, 5 Oct 1837; W. C. Campbell, bm.

Campbell, James & Patsey Clark, 26 Oct 1833; Obediah B. Henderson, bm.

Campbell, John & Sally Brooks, 5 March 1811; Moses Smith, bm.

Campbell, William & Mary Ann Elmore, 13 Apr 1840; John Henderson, bm.

Cavness, Alfred & Eliza Craven, 29 Dec 1838; George Smith, bm.

Caviness, Joab & Elizabeth Mann, 14 March 1818; Barney Fox, bm.

Chamness, William & Margaret Henshaw, 7 Sept 1817; William -----, bm.

Champ, Stephanus & Hannah Curl, 18 Oct 1813; Clabon Guthrie, bm.

Chapman, Deberry & Polly Cross, 12 Aug 1813; Robt. Ragland, bm.

Chavis, James & Nancy Bird, 29 Dec 1812; Pete Chavis, bm.

Chavis, William & Lucinda Archy, 22 Dec 1836; Wm. Ragaland, bm.

Chavous, Thomas & Nancy Chavas, 27 Oct 1827; John Dorset, bm.

Cheek, James & Nancy Shepard, 13 Dec 1833; Jesse Womble, bm.

Cheek, Silas & Edith Philips, 15 Aug 1822; Lazarus Philips, bm.

Christian, Hardy & Ruth Stokes, 4 Nov 1811; John Farrar, bm.

Clark, Elijah & Susan Bynum, 22 March 1840; Jonathan Clark, bm.

Clark, Isaac & Milly Clark, 6 March 1819; Anderson Smith, bm.

Clark, John & Barsheba Dowdy, 1 Oct 1829; John Hargrove, bm.

Clark, Joseph & Elizabeth Tysor, 13 June 1842; Wesley Hanks, bm.

Clark, Thomas & Sarah Webster, (no date, during admn. of Gov. David L. Swain); William Fooshee, bm.

Clawson, William & Kesiah Ward, 16 June 1811; Isaac Marshall, bm.

Clegg, Isaac & Nancy Snipes, 13 Nov 1816.

Coble, Daniel & Polly Vestal, 5 Dec 1827; Robert R. McMath, bm.

Cole, John & Nelly Whitaker, 24 Oct 1839; Redding Person, bm.

Coley, Francis & Sarah Ackman(?), 26 Sept 1808; Elisha Harris, bm.

Collins, William H. & Apphia Williams, 7 Dec 1833; Albert B. Stith, Samuel M. Boylan, bm.

Cooper, William & Jane Ray, _____; Matthew Cooper, bm.

Coulson, Michael & Sarah Pilkinton, 25 Jan 1838; John Brewer, bm.

Council, Emily (sic) & Nancy Lawrence, (no date, during admn. of Gov. Muntford Stokes); John Dowdy, bm.

Cox, Abijah & Sarah Carter, 18 Nov 1820; William Teague, bm.

Cox, John & Mourning Stevens, 10 June 1809; Joseph Jinks, bm.

Craven, Anderson & Betsey Fox, 10 Oct 1819; Nicholas Fox, bm.

Craven, Peter Jr. & Nancy T. Masey, 18 Jan 1846; Alexander S. Masey, bm.

Crayton, George & Fanny Blalock, 10 Feb 1827; Alexander Murcheson, bm.

Croaker, William F. & Neely Ann Archy, 20 Dec 1851; Fadias Stout, bm; m 21 Dec 1851 by S. Stuart.

Crocker, John & Sarah Lineberry, 21 Apr 1852; Reuben Justice, bm; m 21 Apr 1852 by S. Stuart, J. P.

Cross, Richard & Sally Springfield, 14 Feb 1832; Alvin Ragland, bm.

Crutchfield, Benjamin & Elizabeth Clark, 13 Dec 1853; Eli W. Webster, bm.

Crutchfield, James & Diamah Crutchfield, 3 Sept 1831.

Crutchfield, John & Ruth Stout, 3 Feb 1819; Henry Crutchfield, bm.

Crutchfield, John & Sally Williams, 20 March 1827; Richard Cate, bm.

Culberson, John & Peggy Webster, 22 Jan 1811; Samuel Culberson, bm.

Culberson, Joseph & Ann Stenson, 26 Feb 1814; Zadock Barben, bm.

Culberson, William & Mary Brooks, 11 Aug 1821; Parker Brooks, bm.

Curl, James & Jane Wise, 18 Oct 1813; Philip Alston, bm.

Darden, Jacob & Luraner Hill, 15 March 1782; Deberry Chapman, bm.

Dark, Joseph Junr. & Ruth Brooks, 21 Dec 1811; Brooks Brantly, bm.

Dark, Josiah & Susannah Headen, 22 Feb 1817.

Dark, William & Winnafred Dark, 19 Mary 1813; John McGee, bm.

Davis, Allen & Alsa Bullard, 12 Nov 1833; William Crump, bm.

Davis, Jackson & Martha Mason, 8 Apr 1840; John Neal, bm.

Davis, Thomas F. Junr. & Ann J. Moon, 1 Apr 1832; Wm. H. Hardin, bm.

Debrutz, Gabriel & Deborah Montgomery, 13 March 1792; John Montgomery, bm.

Dickens, Anderson & Eliza Hinsley, 4 June 1845.

Dickerson, Wiley & Nancy Cole, 9 Sept 1822; Thomas G. Carter, bm.

Dickin, Andrew J. & Lucinda Woodall, 25 Aug 1850; Zachariah Mann, bm.

Dillard, Elisha & Mary Pope, 10 May 1791; Jesse Daniel, bm.

Dilliard, Joseph J. & Isabella Battle, 21 May 1834; George W. Thompson, bm.

Dixon, Jacob & Nancy Paskill, 19 June 1814; Micajah Elliott, bm.

Dixon, Simon & Elenor Williams, 24 Dec 1829; Simon Hornady, bm.

Dodd, Benjamin & Luvicas Hainy, 1 Jan 1817; Alexander Dodd, bm.

Doller, Jonathan & Sally Williams, 17 June 1840; Tapley Doller, bm.

Dorset, Duty & Rachel Edwards, 12 Sept 1813; Edward Mulloy, bm.

Dorset, Hezekiah & Julia Ann Perry, 9 Feb 1841; James Dowdy, bm.

Dorset, James & Susanna Vestal, 18 Feb 1828; Alexander Murchison, bm.

Dorset, William & Rachel Smith, 1 Sept 1811; Jonathan Smith, bm.

Dorsett, Joseph J. & Catharine Jones, 30 Nov 1842; James Hackney, bm.

Dorsett, Robert & Sarah Perry, 16 Aug 1842; Benjamin Fooshee, bm.

Dorsett, Russell & Susannah Culberson, 20 Sept 1814; Duty Dorset, bm.

Doub, Peter & Elizabeth Brantly, 17 Aug 1821; Thomas G. Carter, bm.

Dowd, Atlas S. & Mary J. Watson, 11 Oct 1841; Calvin D. Bray, bm.

Dowdy, Balaam & Keziah Riddle, 2 May 1806; James Bennett, bm.

Duke, Lew Allen & Sally Crutchfield, 29 Aug 1829; David Stephens, bm.

Duncan, Howard & _____, 1 June 1816; John Reeves, bm.

Duncan, Joab & Hollen Coggin, 26 Dec 1815; John Coggin, bm.

Dungil, William & Rebecca Goin, 4 Oct 1837; John Dungil, bm.

Dunn, Thomas & Margarett G. McHaggrett, 9 July 1862; W. J. Sloan, bm.

Duty, William & Jemimah Edwards, 3 Jan 1811; Edmond Adcock, Wm. Moody, bm.

Eastridge, James & Cynthia Parish, 12 July 1838; George Smith, bm.

Edwards, Charles & Susanah Teague, 3 June 1811; Stokes Edwards, bm.

Edwards, Edom & Mary Bray, 2 Feb 1810; Joshua Edwards, bm.

Edwards, Thomas & Kezziah S. Moody,k 6 Oct 1821; Samuel B. Edwards, bm.

Edwards, W. W. & E. H. (or A.) Fox, 3 Jan 1867; J. N. Edwards, bm.

Elkins, Joel & Sally Harris, 24 Apr 1839; Tarleton Johnson, bm.

Elkins, Lewis & Dicy Lawhorn, 29 Dec 1811; Zadock Barben, bm.

Ellington, Fielding F. & Nancy Lewis, 6 Feb 1834; George W. Ellington, bm.

Ellington, Woodward H. & Gracy Bland, 28 Nov 1833; Wesley Hanks, bm.

Ellis, Allen & Charlotte Thrift, 7 Apr 1838; Atlas J. Baldwin, bm.

Ellis, Andrew & Lucy Wimbley, 25 Feb 1840; Sims Upchurch, bm.

Ellis, Lemul & Tabitha Hatley, 20 Dec 1865, m. 11 Dec 1865 by Dempsey Johnson, J. P.

Ellis, Robert & Elizabeth Wicker, 24 June 1839; Benjamin Wicker, bm.

Ellis, William & Elizabeth Scott, 17 March 1834; Isaiah Neal, bm.

Elmore, Alfred & Elizabeth Clark, 13 Feb 1838; Joseph Elmore, B. W. Carter, bm.

Elmore, John & Caroline Moon, 3 April 1838; Wesley Hanks, bm.

Elmore, Joseph & Elizabeth Self, _____; James Self, bm.

Emmerson, Eli B. & Winny Smith, 11 Nov 1850; James Beal, bm.

Estes, Willie & Amy Hackney, 12 Dec 1813; Young Sellars, bm.

Eubanks, Sidney & Mary Horton, 18 Dec 1852; Joseph B. Lasater, bm.

Euliss, Peter & Jamimy McMath, 12 March 1830; James Wilkison, bm.

Evans, Aaron & Lydia Johnson, 17 Feb 1833; Joseph Johnson, bm.

Evans, Owen & Martha Glass, 13 Sept 1852.

Evans, Shubal & Polly Nelson, 10 Oct 1823; Robert R. McMath, bm.

Faglin (or Foylin), Isaac & Delilah Staly, 7 May 1832; Martin Faglin (or Foylin), bm.

Farrar, George & Candas Wilson, 14 Dec 1840; David Gardner, bm.

Farrar, Obadiah & Sally Avent, 11 March 1840; John B. Drake, bm.

Farrrell, James M. & Matilda Stallings, 12 Jan 1852; m 13 Jan 1852 by Gaston Farrar.

Fearington, John & Bethenea Baldwin, 10 Nov 1817; William Poe, bm.

Ferguson, John & Elizabeth Lutterlok, 12 Nov 1836; Lewis Lutterlok, bm.

Fields, Calvin & Mariah Moody, 23 Dec 1845; John Adcock, bm.

Fields, George & Rebecca Malone, 28 Aug 1839; John Fields, bm.

Fleming, John & Sophia Aldridge, 26 Apr 1817; Alfored Flemings, bm.

Flemings, David & Betsey Edwards, 16 March 1811; Thomas Parks, bm.

Folkner, Sidney & Elizabeth Harriss, 23 May 1839; Owen Lindley, bm.

Fooshee, Charles S. & Mariah Dowd, 13 Nov 1839; William S. Edwards, bm.

Fooshee, Henry & _____ Cole, 25 Sept 1833; Benjamin Horton, bm.

Fooshee, John & Esther Fike, 14 Sept 1812; Kutchen Piĺkenton, bm.

Fooshee, Sidney & Polly Thompson, 4 April 1840; Stanford Petty, bm.

Fooshee, William B. & Martha Straughan, 19 Dec 1836; Joseph Beal, bm.

Forgeson, Tobias & Delilah McPherson, 4 Sept 1832; Reuben Hendricks, bm.

Forester, Samuel & Susan Bray, 5 Dec 1838; Nelson Brady, bm.

Foust, Henry M. & Sarah A. Goldston, 20 July 1850; Joseph J. Goldston, bm.

Fox, George & Sally Teague, 9 Dec 1826; Nicholas Fox, bm.

Fox, Joseph John & Elizabeth Dorsett, 20 Aug 1841; Joseph John Hackney, bm.

Fox, Nicholas & Nancy Johnston, (no date, during admn. of Gov. Gabriel Homes); Robert Henson, bm.

Foylin (or Faglin), Isaac & Delilah Staly, 7 Mayh 1832; Martin Foylin (or Faglin), bm.

Franklin, Henry & Eliza Walker, 26 Apr 1844.

Frazier, Richard & Jane Watson, 17 Nov 1842; John Haughton, bm.

Freeman, Benjamin & Polly Temples, 15 Feb 1814; James Brooks, bm.

Freeman, Lemuel & Rebecca Griffen, 2 Sept 1812; Wm. Emmerson, bm.

Galloway, Mathew Justice & Patsy Beal, 24 Jan 1824; Archibald McIntyre, bm.

Garner, Marshall G. & Sarah Rogers, 29 Apr 1841; Josiah Headen, bm.

Gee, Thomas & Mary Adcock, 16 Jan 1842; George W. Gee, bm.

Gibbs, William & Didama Johnson, 16 March 1819; Joseph Hobson, bm.

Gilbert, William & Elizabeth Hanks or Harris[torn], 24 Dec 1818; Lewis Elkins, bm.

Gilder, Henry & Rebecca Carlisle, 28 Jan 1829; Robert Love, bm.

Gilliam, Jackson & Dilla Boling, 7 Feb 1831; Wesley Hanks, bm.

Gillmore, Samuel & Polly Hart, 15 July 1810; Merrill Hart, bm.

Gilmore, Carny & Sally Buchanan, 6 Dec 1836; Henry C. Burns, bm.

Goldston, George W. & Margaret L. Palmer, 23 May 1831; Joseph J. Goldston, bm.

Goodwin, Calvin & Sally Cotton, 13 Nov 1839; Lorenzo Goodwin, bm.

Goodwin, Hinton & Wilby Hicks, 17 Dec 1842; Thomas Womble, bm.

Goodwin, James & Dilly Hart, 6 July 1817; Merrill Hart, bm.

Goodwin, William & Mary Cotten, 16 Oct 1837; Rhodrick Goodwin, N. A. Stedman, bm.

Graham, James & Eleanor Justice, 4 Aug 1842; David Dixon, bm.

Green, Calvin J. & Martha Barbee, 22 Sept 1851; J. W. B. Lasater, bm.

Griffin, Benjamin Mitchel & Temperance Alston, 28 Jan 1796; William Thompson, Archibald McBride, bm.

Griffin, Samuel & Rebecca Smith, 28 July 1812; Isaac Smith, bm.

Griffis, John & Sally Ragland, 26 March 1814; William Ragland Jr., bm.

Groce, Alvis & Catharine McManus, 8 Feb 1842; John Harman, bm.

Gun, Arnold & Elizabeth Rose, 27 March 1832; Eli Staly, bm.

Gunter, Abner & Silva I. Drake, 20 Sept 1834; Thomas M. C. Prince, bm.

Gunter, Elisha & Mary Burns, 21 Aug 1833; John W. Gunter, Nathan A. Stedman, bm.

Gunter, William & Mary Bland, 4 Dec 1839; Robert Hackney, bm.

Gunter, William W. & Winney Ledbetter, 15 Dec 1847; Calvin Ledbetter, bm.

Guthrie, German & Ruth Harrris, 23 Nov 1831; James C. Guthrie, Nathan A. Stedman, bm.

Guthrie, Hugh B. & Margaret J. Anderson, 26 July 1841; Hugh W. Peoples, bm.

Hackney, Brantley & Eliza J. Brooks, 20 May 1841; Aaron D. Headen, bm.

Hackney, James & Elizabeth Terry, 20 Sept 1842; Joseph Dorsett, bm.

Hackney, John & Mary George, 14 May 1805; Joseph Hackney, bm.

Hackney, John & Milly Dorsett, 3 Oct 1842; James Hackney, bm.

Hackney, Joseph J. & Susanna Dorsett, 20 Feb 1834; Daniel Hackney, bm.

Hadley, Hiram & Louisa J. Carter, 18 May 1833; Boaz Adams, bm.

Hadley, Jonathan & Jane Hollady, 21 Aug 1832; William Hadley, bm.

Hadley, Simon T. & Mary Hadley, 10 Jan 1824; Simon Johnson, bm.

Hamblet, William & Raechel Dismukes, 29 Sept 1812; Elisha Poe, bm.

Hamlet, Sidney S. & Eliza C. Poe, 27 July 1849; W. A. Nash, bm.

Hammock, John & Rachel Sellars, 1 Apr 1791; Robert Edwards, bm.

Harman, Thomas W. & Mary Mann, 4 Dec 1839; James H. Harman, bm.

Harmon, John & Mary E. Marks, 12 Feb 1834; Abner Gunter, bm.

Harper, Robert Goodloe & Ruth Brooks, 17 Sept 1826; Richard Brooks, bm.

Harper, William H. & Susanna Brooks, 15 Aug 1837; Edward Harper, bm.

Harris, Absalom & Mahaly May, 2 Oct 1816; William Glass, bm.

Harris, Cenes & Mahala Johnson, _____; Jehu M. Faulkner, bm.

Harris, James M. & Nancy McPherson, 16 March 1834; Cornelius McPherson, bm.

Harris, Jesse & Hannah Wells, 15 Jan 1824; Robert R. McMath, bm.

Harris, Oscar E. & Agnes Peoples, 25 March 1852; F. John Goldston, bm.

Hart, John & Peggy McDaniel, 15 May 1792; Thomas Hart, bm.

Hart, Merrill & Nancy Clark, 28 June 1818; Thos Clark, William Ragland, bm.

Hatch, Sidney & Annis Pilkinton, 30 Sept 1834; Abraha Pilkinton, bm.

Hatley, Mark & Nancy Mitchell, 16 Sept 1834; William Stone, bm.

Haughton, Lawrence J. & Martha Harris, 27 Feb 1852; m 2 March 1852 by A. F. Olmsted, minister.

Haynes, Herbert & Sarah Parris, 21 Feb 1801; George Dodd, bm.

Hearin, Canady & Beedy Wilson, 5 May 1810; Henry Wilson, bm.

Hearn, Harton & Eliza Williams, 16 Sept 1841; Oliver Bright, bm.

Hearn, John & Betsey Boon, 15 Dec 1830; George Williams, bm.

Hearne, Howel & Jane Davis, 11 May 1852; m 12 May 1852 by Redding Hatley, J. P.

Henderson, Alfred & Cornelia Harris, 21 Sept 1842; Joseph J. Rives, bm.

Henderson, Plesant & Emily Martin, 20 Nov 1833; Wiley Henderson, Thomas Thompson, bm.

Henshaw, Aaron & Hannah Henshaw, 12 March 1810; Jacob Hobson, bm.

Herndon, Ruben & Nancy Jinkins, 5 Nov 1833; Cannon Davis, R. C. Cotton, bm.

Hickman, Elijah & Elizabeth Gothings, 22 July 1823; John Hinshaw, bm.

Hickman, Elijah & Ann Moon, 12 March 1830; Benjamin Hinshaw, bm.

Hicks, Basil H. & Margy Edwards, 12 May 1841; A. B. Marsh, bm.

Hicks, Mathew & Elizabeth Price, 15 Feb 1809; Arthur Weaver, bm.

Hicks, Wesley & Sarah Wilson, 14 April 1842; C. R. Horton, bm.

Hill, William C. & Elizabeth Fooshee, 29 July 1839; William Fike, bm.

Hilliard, Joseph & Eliza Beal, 3 Jan 1852; m 4 Jan 1842 by A. Gaston Headen, J. P.

Hinshaw, Jesse & Hannah Moon, 24 Sept 1817; Josiah Hinshaw, bm.

Hinshaw, Jesse & Letisha Moss, 3 Nov 1823; Robert R. McMath, bm.

Hinshaw, John & Ferribee Richardson, 19 Nov 1823; David Fox, bm.

Hinton, Edwin & Catharine Farish, 30 Aug 1839; Joshua Hackney, bm.

Hobby, William & Beda Herring, 26 Sept 1847.

Hobby, William & Elizabeth Codle, 20 Jan 1840; Hiram Haithcock, bm.

Hobson, Nathan & Rebecca Freeman, 19 March 1808; Wm. Dowdy, bm.

Holliday, Joshua & Elizabeth Turner, 9 Feb 1841; Alfred Glosson, bm.

Hollowell, Hincely & Dilly Neal, 4 Nov 1833; Wesley Oldham, bm.

Holt, Edwin M. & Emmily Parrish, 30 Sept 1828; Samuel L. Holt, bm.

Holt, James P. & Tiresa Holt, 18 Feb 1852; Richard J. Holt, bm; m 19 Feb 1852 by J. C. Wilson.

Holten, Abner & Elizabeth Ann Roe, 20 June 1839; Mariott Robinson, bm.

Hornady, Zachariah & Catherine Hollady, 11 Oct 1829; Wm. Albright, bm.

Horton, Henry & Elizabeth Griffin, 23 Dec 1842; H. J. Stone, bm.

Howard, N. M. & Silbi B. Basham, 2 Dec 1852; Wm. Patterson, bm; m 2 Dec 1852 by Robert Faucette, J. P.

Howell, Robert & Rachal Wilkinson, 13 May 1796; Thomas Ragland, bm.

Hughes, William & Fanny Buckhannan, 3 Aug 185-; Penelton Secaten(?), bm.

Hunt, Esley & Louisa Lutterloh, 16 Dec 1853; John J. Baldwin, bm.

Hutton, William & Caroline Moon, 7 March 1852; Andrew Moon, bm.

Iseley, Balsor & Catharine Fox, 21 Dec 1811; David Fox, bm.

Jean, Franklin & Nancy Right, _____; James A. Griffith, bm.

Jeffers, Henry & Abigail Smith, 19 Apr 1817; Wilson Gilbert, bm.

Jeffryes, Stanford & Martha Windham, 24 Dec 1849; Joseph Thomas, bm.

Jinks, Joseph & Polly Jones, 3 May 1792; Benjamin Drumond, bm.

Johnson, Aaron & _____, _____; Joseph May, bm.

Johnson, Daniel & Charity Holleman, 3 Dec 1842; George Holt, bm.

Johnson, Dan'l & Sarah Harman, 26 Nov 1833; Harris Johnson, bm.

Johnson, David & Elizabeth Stallings, 23 Oct 1841; O. A. Stedman, bm.

Johnson, Herbert & Derucia Gilbert, 8 May 1809; John Cox, Owen Dowd, bm.

Johnson, Isaac & Penney Jones, 17 March 1832; Wm. G. Sadners, bm.

Johnson, James & Winny Moore, _____; Allston Brown, bm.

Johnson, John & Catharine Mitchell, 23 Dec 1833; William Davis, bm.

Johnson, Joseph & Welmit T. Kemp, 24 Aug 1832; Abner B. Marsh, bm.

Johnson, Robert & Louisa Hearn or Hearen, 21 Dec 18--; William Burke, bm.

Johnson, Tarleton & Susan Andrews, 28 Dec 1839; Ezekial Masey, bm.

Johnston, Isaac & Patsey Beverly, 29 Dec 1832; Kiriss(?) Mirich(?), bm.

Johnston, Jacob & Hannah Davidson, 8 May 1816; Joshua Edwards Jr., bm.

Johnston, Jacob & Betsey Gibbs, 6 Feb 1825; William Jordan, John Griffis, bm.

Johnston, Joseh & Rebecca Crutchfield, 1 Jan 1814; Joseph McMath, bm.

Johnston, Micajah & Polly Edards, 30 Nov 1827; Ebenezer Buntyne, bm.

Johnston, Simon & Rebecca McPherson, 15 May 1810; _____ Johnston, bm.

Johnston, Stephen & Elizabeth Johnston, 12 March 1811; Turner Johnston, bm.

Johnston, Stephen & Peggy Teague, 6 May 1812; Hezekiah Dorset, bm.

Jones, James A. & Sally Fields, 15 Feb 1842; Aaron D. Headen, bm.

Jones, Richard Junr. & Fanny Brooks, 30 Dec 1811; Wm. Cox, bm.

Jones, Richmond A. & Agnes W. Johnson, 12 June 1821; Jonathan Cloud, bm.

Jones, Sebourn & Minty Deaton, 18 Aug 1830; Charles Jones, bm.

Jones, William & Sally Culberson, 11 Aug 1827; William Culberson, bm.

Jones, Willis & Elizabeth Gee, 20 Feb 1811; Lewis Jones, bm.

Jopling, James & Rebecca Brewer, _____; John Brewer, bm.

Jordan, Wiatt & Nancy Dark, 29 Oct 1828; John Smith, bm.

Jordan, William & Rebecca Purvis, 19 Aug 1813; Joseph Kempe, bm.

Kelly, Thomas & Elizabeth Wicker, 10 Feb 1840; Frederick Rollins, bm.

Kemp, Jesse & Martha Edwards, 7 Dec 1840; William S. Edwards, bm.

Kemp, Joseph & Dorcas Coshatt, 20 Feb 1812; Thomas Ratcliff, bm.

Kidd, Lewis & Rebecca Brooks, 13 May 1827; Timothy T. Brooks, bm.

King, Cyrus & Cynthia H. Hardin, 17 May 1842; John J. Toomer, bm.

Kinney, Lewis & Nancy Lamb, 6 Sept 1828; Micajah Johnston, bm.

Kinney, William & Sarah Jinkins, 23 Jan 1823; Alexander Hatt, bm.

Kirk, George & Phebe Ramsey, 22 Aug 1812; Samuel Perry, bm.

Lambeth, Thomas & Harriet Sturdivant, 20 Nov 1839; Troy Wilson, bm.

Lane, John S. & Cary Kidd, 9 Oct 1824; Ira Laen, bm.

Lane, Tidenee & Elizabeth Fox, 14 Dec 1817; David Fox son of John Fox, bm.

Lasater, J. B. & Quinnetta Upchurch, 12 Jan 1852; m 15 Jan 1852 by P. W. Dowd.

Lawrence, Thomas & Polly Goodwin, 1 July 1839; Henry Goodwin, bm.

Lea, Joseph & Julia Banks, 14 Apr 1810; Charles Smith, bm.

Leach, John J. A. & Eliza Ann Thompson, 30 Jan 1838; John F. Sanders, bm.

Ledbetter, Chesley & Martha Siler, 10 Sept 1824; Lem'l S. McNiell, bm.

Lee, Woodson & Elizabeth Prince, 23 Dec 1816; Rhoderick Cotten, bm.

Lennens, James & Elizabeth Thompson, 14 Feb 1811; Young Sellers, bm.

Lewis, James & Martha Workman, 21 June 1834; R. C. Cotten, bm.

Lineberry, John & Rachel Edwards, 21 June 1834; Isham Man, bm.

Lineberrry, Mackling & Hester Staly, 7 June 1832; John Ingold, bm.

Lindsey, Norris & Anna Price, 8 Jan 1833; Oliver Brewer, bm.

Little, John & Nancy Bright, 30 May 1833; Robert Bingham, Wesley Hanks, bm.

Long, William A. & Nancy Horton, 20 April 1833; William Hollowell, bm.

Lynch, Caswell & Keziah Lynch, 24 Dec 1831; A. T. Bowlin, bm.

Lynch, William & Ruth T. Pearce, _____; Eli Fogleman, bm.

CHATHAM COUNTY NC MARRIAGES 1772-1868

Lyneberry, James & Ann Greaves, 26 Jul 1810; Thomas Greaves or Graves, bm.

McBain, Daniel & Hannah Quakenbush, 6 Jan 1840; John Guthrie, bm.

McCall, John & Darios Coshall, 20 July 1812; Joseph Kemp, bm.

McClelland, Malcom & Polly Staly, 8 Jan 1831; David Pickett, bm.

McCollum, Isaac & Susannah McMasters, 16 Aug 1811; Zacharias Cox, bm.

McCoy, Paschal C. & Elizabeth Owen, 26 Oct 1837; William McCoy, bm.

McDaniel, Joseph & Lucy Bright, 11 Nov 1813; Alsey Ledbetter, bm.

McDonald, Phileman H. & Susannah Lasater, 24 Sept 1811; George Drake, bm.

McGee, John & Milly Dark, 7 June 1813; Brooks Brantly, bm.

McGilvary, John M. & Ellen McIver, 18 Oct 1837; Rhoderick McIntosh, bm.

McIntosh, Murdock & Keddy Stallings, 8 May 1816; Daniel Thompson, bm.

McIver, Danl. or R. & Isabella McIver, 24 Aug 1819; R. or Danl. McIver, bm.

McIver, Rhoderick A. & Maria Tysor, 10 Feb 1840; Aaron Tilman, bm.

McIver, Robert & Elizabeth Wicker, 5 Sept 1838; John McIver, John Harman, bm.

McKevor, David & Eliza Ran Patterson, 9 Aug 1831; Wm. Carlisle, bm.

McLean, Daniel & Teretia Utly, 5 Apr 1828; John H. Hawkins, bm.

McManus, Nathan D. & Mary Jane Stinson, 11 Feb 1839; Jesse Womble, bm.

McMaster, Samuel & Eleanor Hadly, 13 Apr 1812; John McMasters, bm.

McMath, James & Polly Johnson, 24 May 1814; Hiram Wright, bm.

McMath, Robert R. & Mimy Vestal, 3 Nov 1823; Jesse Hinshaw, bm.

McPherson, Aron & Charity Johnston, 2 Oct 1824; William McPherson, bm.

McPherson, Daniel & Rachel Goshall, 18 Sept 1821; James McPherson, bm.

McPherson, Duncan & Polly Dark, 2 Jan 1832; David McPherson, bm.

McPherson, John & Mary Lindley, 17 March 1834; William McPherson, bm.

McPherson, Oliver & Malinda Lamb, 27 Apr 1852; Wm. P. McDaniel, bm.

McPherson, Stephen & Patience Holliday, 13 Feb 1819; Willis Dark, bm.

McPherson, Stephen W. & Caty Pope, 19 Dec 1828; Jesse Crutchfield, bm.

McPherson, William & Sarah Thomas, 13 June 1812; Elisha Braxton, bm.

McPherson, William & Mary Johnston, 6 Nov 1819; Willis Dark, bm.

McPherson, William & Nancy A. Dark, 22 Jan 1839; William Albright, bm.

Maddox, Calven & Semanthy Buchanon, 10 Feb 1842; Green Womack, bm.

Malone, Claiborne & Cathrine Smith, 3 Sept 1833; Jacob Johnson, bm.

Malone, Samuel & Ann Scarborough, 24 Apr 1824; William A. Rives, bm.

Mann, Jesse G. & Elizabeth Perry, 4 May 1832; F. A. Mann, bm.

Marcum, William & Nancy Mason, 3 May 1842; Bennet Bachelor, bm.

Marks, Richard S. & Martha A. Minten, 22 Nov 1845; N. A. Stedman, bm.

Marks, Zacheus, & Emaline Burns, 10 Dec 1842; Micajah Burns, bm.

Marley, David & Mariah Culbertson, 23 July 1833; Calvin Vestal, bm.

Marshall, Jonathan & Eunice Hadley, 28 Sept 1842; John Guthrie, bm.

Marshall, Joseph & Sarah Newland, __ Aug 1817.

Martin, Sidney & Peggy Love(?), 12 Jan 1832; Stephen Robeson, Merrill Robeson, bm.

Mathas, Hardy & May Davis, 11 June 1849; John Mathas, Wesley Hicks, bm.

Mathis, Thomas & Mary Rutherford, 16 Apr 1772; Deberry Chapman, bm.

Maynard, Jacob & Elizabeth Harwood, 23 Dec 1842; John Maynard, bm.

Millican, William & Nancy Ramsey, 27 Oct 1814; Elias Millican, bm.

Mims, B. W. & Mary A. Farrar, 17 Nov 1839; David Gardner, bm.

Minter, Abner H. & Charity Chapman, 6 July 1809; Richard Minter, bm.

Mitchel, William & Easter Ann Rigsby, 10 Oct 1850; Jesse B. Penney, bm.

Mitchell, James C. & Caroline Lightfoot, 18 May 1828; Nathan A. Stedman, bm.

Mitchell, Kelly & Celia Horton, 15 March 1842; Timri Riggbee, bm.

Mitchell, Ransford & Eleanor Lewis, 27 Sept 1808; Oliver Prince, bm.

Mobley, Andrew & Polly Teague, 13 Feb 1839; Uriah Hinson, bm.

Moffitt, Adam & Elizabeth Bray, 16 Aug 1819; Edward Bray, bm.

Moffitt, Elijah W. & Sally Vestal, 20 Aug 1832; Christian Ritsman, bm.

Moody, Elisha & Milley Thomason, 11 Feb 1827; Balaam Thomason, bm.

Moody, Joel & Gilly Moody, 15 Sept 1819; Riley Moody, bm.

Moon, George & Mary Bray, 16 Jan 1819; John Moon, bm.

Moon, Jesse & Elizabeth Stout, 20 Apr 1816; Thomas Hinshaw, bm.

Moon, John & Elizabeth Crutchfield, 13 Jan 1818; Moses Adams, bm.

Moon, John & Agnes F. Hat, 8 March 1834; Jesse Smith, bm.

Moon, Jonathan & Hannah Lynch, 26 Dec 1820; Simon Moon, bm.

Moon, Joseph & Fanny Bray, 18 March 1818; Edward Bray, bm.

Moon, Joshua & Margarett Fox, 7 May 1818; Jonathan Moon, bm.

Moon, William & Susannah Hancock, 7 June 1813; Joseph Moon, bm.

Moon, William & Phebe Stout, 16 June 1832; Zimri Vestal, bm.

Moore, Alexander H. & Eleanor F. Prince, 25 March 1834; Alexander H. Dismukes, Wesley Hicks, bm.

Moore, William & Martha Cummings, 25 Sept 1833; John D. Fooshee, bm.

Morris, Fielding & Hannah Cook, (no date, during admn. of Gov. Muntfort Stokes); William Mitchell, bm.

Morris, James & Mary Pilkinton, 7 June 1834; Abraham Pilkinton, bm.

Munden, John & Peggy L. Johnson, 21 Aug 1827; Peter P. Smith, bm.

Myrick, Azel & Fanny Tucker, 31 July 1811; Benjamin Smith, bm.

Myrick, Harris & Amey Johnston, 25 May 1815; Josiah Moody, bm.

Myrick, Ransom & Peggy Jolly, 20 Oct 1801; Bolling Jolly, bm.

Nall, John & Nancy Brady, 4 April 1818; Josiah Glass, bm.

Neal, Stephen & Elizabeth Poe, 17 Feb 1782; Stephen Neil, Prettymon Berry, bm.

Nelson, Jefferson & Hannah _____, 31 March 1827; George Smith, bm.

Nelson, Jesse & Ruth Temple, 16 May 1830; David Coble, bm.

Nelson, Samuel & Merris Aldred, 15 July 1821; Benjamin Hinshaw, bm.

Nevill, Matthew & Mahala Kerby, 6 Oct 1828; Manly Snipes, bm.

Newby, Solomon & Margaret Benton, 25 May 1830; Larkin Nicholson, bm.

Newlin, Jehu & Hannah Hadley, 23 Sept 1840; James J. Graham, bm.

Nicholson, Cornelius & Mary Ann Palmer, 18 Dec 1833; Oran A. Palmer, bm.

Nicholson, Donald & Christie McInnis, 2 Jan 1818; Miles McInnis, bm.

Nicholson, Larkin & Rebecca Barton, 24 Sept 1828; James Ginn, bm.

Night, Neal & Martha Jean, 14 Feb 1842; Samuel Brasington, bm.

Norwood, John & Spicy Mann, 8 Nov 1829; Francis Dowd, bm.

Norwood, John & Martha Snipes, 1 Jan 1838; William Snipes, bm.

Norwood, Mitchell & Sarah Piggott, 21 Sept 1836; Sylvanus Perry, bm.

O'Daniel, James & Polly Marsh, 31 Jan 1815; Henry Dorsett, bm.

Oldham, David & Caroline McDaniel, 4 March 1842; John Hart, bm.

Oldham, Ephraim & Jane Neal, 27 March 1840; Henry Oldham, bm.

Oldham, Wesley & Nancy Mason, 3 Dec 1839; Pleasant Merritt, bm.

Olive, Anderson of Wake County, & Emeline Ester Ann Florentine
Yarbrough, 22 Jan 1852; m 29 Jan 1852 by Johnson Olive,
minister.

Overman, John & Marian Evans, 31 Oct 1823; Benjamin Way, bm.

Overman, Manliff & Rebecca Bunting, 28 Aug 1852; Hezekiah
Overman, bm.

Owen, Evan F. & Celia Mann, 15 Dec 1840; Enoch Williams, bm.

Owen, Thomas & Tynerah Hearin, 5 Apr 1810; John Wilson, bm.

Pace, James & Elizabeth Hackney, 24 Oct 1851; S. L. Riddle, bm; m
26 Oct 1851 by Wm. Lineberry, M. G.

Palmer, James M. & Sophia M. Lutterloh, 2 Jan 1840; Edwin A.
Hearitt, bm.

Parish, David & Milly Fox, 1 Nov 1842; William Smith, bm.

Parish, Goode & Priscilla Richards, 17 Feb 1813; John Herndon, bm.

Partin, Aldridge J. & Mary T. Hearn, 20 Dec 1842; Daniel Tillman,
bm.

Partridge, John & Patsey Booker, 12 May 1812; Frederick Ragland,
bm.

Pascall, Richard & Nancy Bray, 24 Aug 1817; William Moody, bm.

Patterson, David & Sally Headen, 21 Feb 1829; John Patterson, bm.

Patterson, George D. & Mary Blackston, 30 Oct 1840; William
Flinton, bm.

Patterson, William & Leah P. Dowd, 2 March 1828; Samuel Hynn(?),
bm.

Pattishall, Benjamin R. & Emeline Lawrence, 1 Feb 1853; Rhodes Pattishall, bm.

Pearson, Hardy & Elizabeth Brewer, 8 Jan 1840; Benjamin Williams, bm.

Pennington, John & Jane Garner, 19 March 1838; Thomas B. Clark, bm.

Perry, Abner & Sarah McPherson, 13 Aug 182; Samuel H. Crutchfield, bm.

Perry, James Junr. & Hannah Rives, 24 Sept 1822; Henry Lutterloh, bm.

Perry, Samuel Junr. & Julia Stone, 16 Dec 1828; George R. Griffith, bm.

Perry, Wesley & Winney A. Burns, 19 Aug 1839; Robert H. Green, bm.

Perry, William & Ann Baldwin, 17 Feb 1813; Peter Perry, bm.

Petteford, Edmon & Salley Carter, 23 Dec 1816; Jonathan Carter, bm.

Pettey, Allen & Jane Richerson, 13 Oct 1859; m 13 Oct 1859 by A. Glasson, J. P.

Petty, George D. & Sally Teague, 22 Aug 1826; Joseph F. Stone, bm.

Petty, Guildord & Sally Harrington, 10 Oct 1812; Raford Petty, bm.

Petty, John & Delilah Clark, 13 June 1834; Joseph Fooshee, Stephen Petty, bm.

Petty, Joseph & Zaney Fooshee, 22 Feb 1817; Daniel Fooshee, bm.

Petty, Morris & Jane Brasington, 18 Aug 1851; m 24 Aug 1851 by Littlejohn Utley.

Petty, Stanford & Nancy Self, 12 Oct 1833; Bluford Petty, bm.

Petty, Stephen & Matilda Boon, 23 June 1833; Thomas Thompson, bm.

Petty, Stephen & Patsey Howell, 26 July 1834; James Hamblet, bm.

Philips, Alfred & Sophia Siler, 1 Nov 1837; William Adcock, bm.

Phillip, Noah & Emily J. Beal, 8 March 1853; Orvon Andrews, bm.

Phillips, Laban & Lydia McManus, 25 Feb 1835; Benjamin McManus, om.

Phillips, Lindsey & Dorcas Nall, 14 Sept 1812; Joshua Glass, bm.

Phillips, Sanders & Sally Perry, 30 Dec 1834; John Cheek, bm.

Phillips, Thomas & Dilly Beal, 13 Sept 1810; Merrell Hart, bm.

Piggott, Isaiah & Phebe McMaster, 9 Oct 1812; John McMasters, bm.

Pilkenton, John & Temperance Hally, 11 June 1822; Daniel Brown, bm.

Pilkinton, Abram & Rena Durham, 7 Oct 1834; Sydney Hatch, bm.

Poe, Thomas & Elizabeth Neal, 12 Sept 1851; John Poe, bm.

Poe, Willis & Frances Hackny, 20 Dec 1830; William Dowdy, bm.

Pope, Richard & Patsey Pichard(?), 23 Oct 1830; Jesse Hinshaw, bm.

Pounds, Lewis & Peggy Johnston, 13 Oct 1813; Isham Mann, bm.

Pounds, William & Jane Hadley, 15 Apr 1815; Isham Mann, bm.

Powell, James R. & Nancy Aldridge, (no date, during admn. of Gov. Muntfort Stokes); Charles Powell, bm.

Powell, Thos & Nancy Bradors, (no date, during admn. of Gov. Muntfort Stokes); John Justice, bm.

Price, Lindsey & Elizabeth Petty, 4 Feb 1817; Isaac Petty, bm.

Pritchett, Eason & Gillico Woods, 31 May 1839; Jonathan Dollar, bm.

Pugh, John A. & Mary L. Beal, 21 Sept 1852.

Purvis, George & Milly Jourdan, 4 Feb 1816; Samuel Elkins, Isham ____, bm.

Quakenbush, Jacob & Ruthy McPherson, 15 Jan 1813; Thomas Dark, bm.

Ragland, Frederick W. & Sally Glass, 17 July 1810; Wm. Ragland, bm.

Ragland, William & Martha T. Edwards, 6 May 1812; William Glass, bm.

Rains, John & Jane Cox, 11 Nov 1820; Francis Dorset, bm.

Rains, William & Elizabeth Sanders, 17 Jan 1821; Francis Dorset, bm.

Rawnsley, Jonas & Polly Craton, 20 Oct 1836; Abrahm Houdley, bm.

Ray, Pinckney & Margaret Burns, 5 Dec 1851; m 7 Dec 1851 by Wm. Lineberry, M. G.

Ray, Rittenhouse & Susan Patterson, 11 Feb 1841; Ira Rosson, bm.

Record, Adam & Sally Forrester, 18 Sept 1811; John Carter Junr., bm.

Redfern, Isaac & Winey Hughs, 38 March 1819; John Dean, bm.

Richardson, Edmund & Hannah Williams, 21 Jan 1824; John Buckner, bm.

Richardson, Hardeman & Ann Pilkington, 18 Aug 1801; John Pilkenton, bm.

Riddle, Anderson & Lydia Bunn, 8 Dec 1812; William Scurlock, bm.

Riddle, Cato & Patty Tommolin, 13 Feb 1782; Whitmill Harrington, bm.

Riddle, Cato & Nancy Hagood, 9 Dec 1812; William Riddle, bm.

Riggsbee, Thomas & Elizabeth Bennett, 16 March 1841; Young Oldham, bm.

Rivers, Jones & Sally Underwood, 28 Jan 1824; Augustine Rose, bm.

Rives, George & Mary Crutchfield, 10 March 1842; Joseph J. Rives, bm.

Rives, James F. & Elizabeth A. Marsh, 21 Jan 1842; John P. Rives, bm.

Rives, John & Nancy Brooks, 20 May 1811; Larkin Brooks, bm.

Rives, Reuben & Hannah Kirk, 22 Apr 1812; William Clark, bm.

Roberson, David & Sally Snipes, __ July 1825; John Justice, Nathl. Roberson, bm.

Roberson, Stephen & Eliza Edwards, 8 Feb 1834; Merritt Roberson, bm.

Roberts, James & Polly Stewart, 12 Feb 1822; Thomas Cottrell, bm.

Roberts, Richard & ____ Bird, 14 Dec 1827; John Archy, bm.

Roberts, Thomas & Eliza Phillips, 26 March 1840; John Adcock, bm.

Robertson, Henry & Delilah Campbell, 11 July 1828; Stephen Robertson, bm.

Rogers, Jesse & Mahaly Crutchfield, 27 March 1832; Bluford Petty, bm.

Rogers, John & Joanna Lutterloh, 9 Jan 1852; m 13 Jan 1852 by L. Burnett, minister.

Ronslew, James & Margaret McPherson, 13 July 1832; Zachariah Kornagay, bm.

Rosser, Joseph & Nancy Burke, 2 Jan 1840; H. H. Burke, bm.

Rosson, Hiram & Sarah Hopson, 9 Jan 1817; Jesse Rosson, bm.

Rosson, Hiram & Frances Chamness, 15 Feb 1817; Josiah Whitehead, bm.

Rosson, Ira & Sarah Wright, 9 Jan 1813; James Wright, bm.

Rosson, William M. & Peggy Edwards, 18 Jan 1839; William Purviss, bm.

Russell, David & Susan Lewis, 1 aug 1839; Wesley Hanks, bm.

Rutherford, John & Jane Riddle, 26 Apr 1817; Thomas Ragland Senr., bm.

Ryan, William & Milly Pilkinton, 10 Jan 1840; John M. Pilkinton, bm.

Sanders, James & Martha Gilmore, 30 Sept 1845; Robert Lambert, bm.

Sanford, James & Anna Snipes, 1 Nov 1816; Beverly Guthrie, bm.

Seamoore, Henry & Betty Herndon, 17 Feb 1782; Robert Carlile, bm.

Seamore, Joseph & Milly Johnson, 16 Jan 1841; Neal Night, bm.

Sears, William & Hannah Dodd, 11 March 1817; Alexander Dodd, bm.

Self, William & Rachel Davidson, 18 Jan 1812; Wm. Moody, bm.

Selph, James & Christian Johnston, 21 Apr 1834; Richard C. Cotten, bm.

Seymour, Isaac & Polly Dickens, 29 Oct 1839; John Seymour, bm.

Sherding, John & Delila Gillum, 16 June 1821; Solomon Stuart, bm.

Siler, Elisha & Sally Thompson, 17 Oct 1810; Isham Mann, bm.

Siler, James & Nancy Jones, 9 July 1834; Chesley Ledbetter, bm.

Siler, John & Agness W. McNeill, 20 Apr 1812; Peter P. Smith, bm.

Siler, Phillip & Peggey Vestal, 18 Aug 1832; Alfred Vestal, bm.

Siler, William D. & Maria Dorset, 9 March 1829; Simri Carter, bm.

Sloan, Alexander & Disa Hartsatte, 19 March 1833; Reddek Burns, bm.

Sloan, Robert & Ann Marks, 15 Jan 1834; Johnson Sloan, Wesley Hanks, bm.

Smith, Alfred & Charlotte C. Lutterloh, 24 Jan 1853; Washington Lutterloh, bm.

Smith, Alston & Catharine Hadley, 2 June 1832; William Perry, bm.

Smith, Ambrose & Elizabeth Ferrell, 28 June 1815; Richard Jones, bm.

Smith, Anderson & Mary Clark, 5 Dec 1810; Micajah Duncan, bm.

Smith, Benjamin & Mary Phillips, 10 Feb 1816; William Miller, Anderson Smith, bm.

Smith, Benjamin & Easter Argo, 21 July 1816; Jacob Teague, bm.

Smith, Eli & Rebecca Stinson, 2 Jan 1821; Robert Stinson Jun., bm.

Smith, James S. & Delia Jones, 18 Oct 1813; Ruffen Jones, bm.

Smith, John & Rebecca Younger, 21 Apr 1818; William Smith, bm.

Smith, Joseph & Matilda Petty, 17 Oct 1842; James G. Marsh, bm.

Smith, Martin & Nancy Ivey, 21 Jan 1839; Atlas A. Burnett, bm.

Smith, Oliver & Charlotte Lewis, 22 June 1841; William Clark, bm.

Smith, Parish & Milly Brown, 11 Feb 1817; James Gillam, bm.

Smith, Thomas & Hannah Hartsal, 12 Sept 1828; Presley Straughan, bm.

Smith, Thomas H. & Nancy Lea, 8 Aug 1810; Joseph Lea, bm.

Snipes, Jesse & Polly Colur, 17 Oct 1813; Mark Snipes, bm.

Snipes, Walter & Nancy Horton, 17 Aug 1842; Lucian Burnett, bm.

Sparrow, William & Mariah Williams, 15 Feb 1841; Jones Morgan, bm.

Stafford, Barnet & Elizabeth Straughan, 1 Nov 1839; Richard Webster, bm.

Staley, George & Polly Siler, 11 Dec 1827; John Staley, bm.

Staley, Wm. H. & Abigail Hinshaw, 16 March 1839; Lewis Albright, bm.

Staly, Eli & Zilphy Rose, 21 Apr 1828; Conrad Staly, bm.

Starr(?), Henry & Nancy Smith, 18 July 1829; Eli Smith, bm.

Stedman, J. M. & Sally Dowdy, 16 Jan 1838; James N. Crosby, bm.

Stedman, John W. & Mary Burns, 23 Feb 1828; Henry Burns, bm.

Stedman, Oran A. & Mary Johnston, 16 Jan 1831; Nathan A. Stedman, bm.

Steel, Thomas & Susannah Overman, 10 Nov 1832; John Patterson, bm.

Stephens, David & Elenoir Green, 28 July 1829; John Hobson, bm.

Stone, Carney & Dilla Jinkins, 13 Jan 1841; H. Jackson Stone, bm.

Stone, David & Ecameliza Willet, 17 March 1841; Aaron Evans, bm.

Stone, Jesse & Phebe Willet, 31 Dec 1826; Joshua Willet, Thomas Beal, Peter Sinclair, bm.

Stout, William & Franky Canter, 24 Dec 1828; Jones Canter, bm.

Straughan, Carney & Lydia Avent, 15 Dec 1841; Solomon D. Crutchfield, bm.

Straughan, Fielding & Mary Poe, 16 March 1842; Wm. T. Horne, bm.

Straughan, John & Mary H. Fooshee, 12 Sept 1852; Elijah F. Lambert, bm.

Straughan, John & Sally Daughordy, 18 Dec 1839; Hadley Johnson, bm.

Strong, William H. & Sarah Moore, 29 Sept 1831.

Swing, John & Elizabeth Hinshaw, 22 Nov 1832; William Wilson, bm.

Talley, Abraham & Polly Dunken, 17 Sept 1810; Wm. Emmerson, bm.

Teague, Eli & Elizabeth Thompson, 13 Sept 1824; Balaam W. S. Thompson, bm.

Teague, Solomon & Peggy McMasters, 19 Oct 1822; Nicholas Bridges, bm.

Teague, William & Ann Carter, 20 Nov 1810; John Culberson, bm.

Teague, William & Anna Caviness, 26 May 1839; Ransom Caviness, bm.

Temple, Green G. & Amy Petty, 12 Sept 1838; William C. Campbell, bm.

Temple, Joseph & Rebecca Nalls, 15 Feb 1842; Tarleton Johnson, bm.

Temples, William & Rebecca Moody, 13 Nov 1827; Jones Moody, bm.

Thomas, Alexander & Nancy Hadley, 13 Apr 1840; Edmond Perry, bm.

Thomas, George & Seloma Marks, 8 Apr 1828; Ewel Marks, bm.

Thomas, Jehu & Jane Campbell, 21 Feb 1853; William Way, bm.

Thomas, John & Elizabeth Stuart, 15 Apr 1853; John Way, bm.

Thomas, William & Judy Rush, 1 Feb 1816; Robert Farras, bm.

Thomason, Balaam & Polly Freeman, 25 Sept 1821; James Brooks, bm.

Thomason, William Junior & Polly Morand, 6 Feb 1813; William Moody, bm.

Thompson, Archy & Lucinda White, 19 Sept 1837; Lary Stith, bm.

Thompson, James & Lydia B. Brooks, 28 Dec 1818; Thomas G. Carter, bm.

Thompson, James & Polly Mann, 25 Aug 1822; John Thompson, bm.

Thompson, John & Susanna Andrews, 1 June 1778; John Montgomery, bm.

CHATHAM COUNTY NC MARRIAGES 1772-1868

Thompson, John & Elizabeth Forrester, 4 Dec 1813; John Davidson, bm.

Tillman, Joseph & Winney Fields, 30 Apr 1811; John Tilman, bm.

Tinnin, John W. & Frances Small, 1 Oct 1851; W. P. Taylor, bm.

Tomlinson, Richard of Randolph County, & Anne Waddill, daughter of Thomas & Margaret Waddill, 11 Nov 1813; Thos Waddill, bm.

Turner, Joseph L. & Frances Rosson, 25 Feb 1820; Joseph J. Brock, bm.

Underwood, Benjamin & Charity Wells, 29 Aug 1811; Allen Jones, bm.

Upchurch, Isham S. & Delia Beavers, 22 Dec 1851; m 23 Dec 1851 by E. P. Fearrington, J. P.

Upchurch, John & Happy Shaw, 28 March 1815; Stephen Petty, bm.

Upchurch, Kelly & Sarah Jane Eason, 19 Sept 1837; William Goodwin, bm.

Upchurch, Sidney & Delia Williams, 6 Oct 1841; David P. Williams, bm.

Utly, Jacob W. & Grissy Ann Buchanon, 6 March 1851; Witty Buchanon, bm.

Valentine, William R. & Mary P. Stone, 2 Feb 1826; Thomas Powell, bm.

Vestal, Andrew & Eliza Dorset, 28 Feb 1828; Archibald Furgeson, bm.

Vestal, Enos & Milly Womble, 16 Nov 1833; Enos B. Johnson, bm.

Vestal, John & Polly Wood, 20 Feb 1824; Rufus McMasters, bm.

Vestal, John & Elizabeth Johnson, 16 Aug 1837; John S. Lane, bm.

Waite, Robert & Sarah Warren, 27 Nov 1808; Peter P. Smith, bm.

Walker, Coleman & Peggy Thrift, 15 Nov 1813; Perry Thrift, bm.

Walker, David & Ferreby Johnston, 17 Oct 1814; William Walker, bm.

Wallace, Warren & Jane Adcock, 24 Jan 1840; Edmund L. Fitts, bm.

Warren, Benjamin & Gemima Bright, 15 Jan 1817; Daniel Fooshie, bm.

Watson, Benjamin & Amanda J. Womble, 1 March 1842; Atlas Dowd, bm.

Watson, David & Happy Burns, 23 Jan 1818; Edmond Welch, bm.

Way, Stanford & Tempy Coble, 20 Dec 1851; D. H. Albright, bm.

Webb, William & Sinai Glosson, 26 Nov 1828; Archibald Perret, bm.

Weber, Henrie & Margaret J. Walker, 17 July 1852; m 18 July 1852 by A. F. Olmsted, minister.

Webster, Henry & Mary Spearman, 24 Dec 1810; William Moody, bm.

Webster, Jesse & Jane Buchner(?), (no date, during admn. of Gov. Muntfort Stokes); James Webster, bm.

Webster, Richard & Sarah Auld, 1 Sept 1834; Simon F. Webster, bm.

Welch, Henry & Polly Hill, 16 March 1819; John Hill, bm.

Wells, Isaac & Mary Pounds, 12 March 1822; Bishop Barker, bm.

Whitehead, Arthur & Elizabeth Crutchfield, 9 March 1833; James Whitehead, bm.

Whitehead, Jacob & Hannah Cox, 11 June 1810; Solomon Underwood, bm.

Whitehead, Josiah & Lydia Foster, 8 Aug 1819; Hezekiah Dorest, bm.

Whitehead, William & Ann Andrew, 15 Nov 1828; John Andrew, bm.

Wicker, Benjamin & Susannah Parish, 19 Dec 1823; John Whitehead, bm.

Wilkerson, Thomas & Hannah Stinson, 12 May 1811; Zebulon Wilkerson, bm.

Wilkie, George T. & Mary Gillam, 6 June 1816; William Wilkie, bm.

Willet, Charles & Amanda Lawhorn, 16 March 1852; m 18 March 1852 by C. Shields, J. P.

Willett, John & Gilly Thomason, 23 ___ 1812; William Moody, bm.

Willet Oran & Phebe Willett, 19 Jan 1842; Asa Beal, bm.

Willet, Ransom & Reeny Brown, 21 Nov 1833; William T. Brooks, bm.

Williams, Andrew B. & Martha Edwards, 25 March 1852; m 25 March 1852 by Wm. M. Rossen, J. P.

Williams, John A. & Emeline Haralson, 4 Dec 1833; Richardson Faucett, bm.

Williams, Riley & Love Carter, 11 Jan 1839; Nathan S. Williams, bm.

Williams, Thomas & Ann Horton, 25 Aug 1833; William Thomas, bm.

Williams, William & _____, ___ 181-; James Caudle, bm.

Williams, William & Polly Moon, 11 Dec 1811; Frederick Tyson, bm.

Williams, William H. & Apphia Taylor, (no date, during admn. of Gov. David L. Swain); John J. Alston, bm.

Wilson, Philip & Lydia B. Carroll, 23 Jan 1835; E. W. Carroll, bm.

Wilson, Samuel & Lucy Richardson, 14 Aug 1810; Oliver Prince, bm.

Womble, Elisha & Kitty Crane, 1 Nov 1851; Noel Williams, bm.

Womble, John D. & Lydia Dowd, 10 Feb 1827; Henry McKenzie, bm.

Womble, Joseph & Mary Fox, 22 Nov 1851; James Welch, bm.

Womble, Neal & Susannah Lambeth, 4 Oct 1819; William Bell, bm.

Wood, Jesse & Leah Brown, 8 Aug 1831; John Brewer, bm.

Woody, Hugh & Elizabeth Cheuss(?), 4 May 1830; Eli Fogleman, bm.

Workman, Thomas & Candas Straughan, 10 Dec 1842; Aderson Gean, bm.

Wright, Andrew & Nancy Crutchfield, 22 Apr 1833; John Cole, bm.

Wright, Andrew & Ruth Johnston, 18 March 1834; Allen Goodwin, bm.

Yates, Carless & Mary Ann Marcom, 17 Dec 1839; William Marcom, bm.

Yates, Simeon & Martha Upchurch, 28 Jan 1840; Cordy Martin, bm.

Yeargin, Hillory & Catharine McGee, 28 Apr 1832; Henry Ward, John J. Goodwin, bm.

Younger, John C. & Betteried(?) Turner, (no date, during admn. of Gov. Muntfort Stokes; William Cooper, bm.

Jacob Utley & Griza J. Buchannon, m 16 Mar 1851 by Thos Ragland, J. P.

Robt Crayton & Mariah Fooshee, m 12 June 1851 by A. D. Toomer, J. P.

W. H. Hughes & Jacobine Averit, m 23 Apr 1851 by Elias Bryant, J. P.

Alfred M. Furgerson & Pyrena E. Vestal, m 1 June 1851 by S. G. Evans.

Josiah C. Foster & Sarah E. Borrow, m 8 June 1851 by S. G. Evans.

John McDaniel & Margaret Moon, m 26 June 1851 by S. G. Evans.

Adam M. Record & Hannah J. Carter, m 19 July 1851 by Wm. Lineberry, Baptist minister, at the house of Samuel Carter.

William Owen & Elizabeth Brown, m 30 July 1851 by J. W. Tinnin, minister.

Alvice A. Nelson & Mary Ann Buckner, m 27 July 1851 by S. G. Evans.

Daniel C. Harden & Efreann C. Harman, m 29 July 1851 by J. W. Tinnin, minister.

Luke Bynum & Nicy Williams, m 8 Aug 1851 by Thomas Lambeth, J. P.

John A. Hanks & Catharine B. Walker, m 2 July 1851 by L. Burnett, minister.

W. M. Burns & Eliza A. Hocks, m 16 Aug 1849 by Jordan Tysor, J. P.

Wright Haithcock & Rosannah Richardson, m 8 June 1851 by Manly Snipes, J. P.

J. C. Cotton & Charlotte Mann, m 31 July 1851 by Manly Snipes, J. P.

Spencer L. Riddle & Louisa A. Drake, m 24 Aug 1851 by W. P. Taylor, minister.

Morris Petty & Jane Brasington, m 17 Aug 1851 by Littlejohn Utley, minister.

Duncan Myrick & Hannah Pritchett, m 1 June 1851 by J. Mann, J. P.

Wm. Lasater & Jane Mitchell, m 25 Aug 1851 by Thomas Lambeth, J. P.

Green Haitchcock & Mary Coose, m 24 Aug 1851 by A. G. Hinton, J. P., at the house of Flat Coose.

Thomas Poe & Elizabeth Neal, m 14 Sept 1851 by J. Williams, J. P.

Cratus Allen & Mary Hatwood, m 28 June 1851 by S. Stuart, J. P.

Riley Lineberry & Clara Hatwood, m 9 March 1851 by S. Stuart, J. P.

William M. Johnson & Augusta Lindley, m 1 May 1851 by Wm. Albright.

George W. Staley & Eliza Wells, m 17 Aug 1851 by Sherbut G. Evans.

W. A. McLennan & Gracy F. Lea, m 7 Oct 1851 by W. P. Taylor, minister.

Orpheus Hannah & Margaret Goldstone, m 7 Oct 1851 by W. P. Taylor, minister.

Julian Straughan & Eliza Bocame, m 17 July 1851 by Richard Webster, J. P.

John Brown & Elizabeth Straughan, m 17 July 1851 by Richard Webster, J. P.

Henry C. Suther & Elizabeth Jane Teague, m 16i Sept 1851 by Wm. Lineberry, minister.

Revd. John W. Tinnin & Frances J. Small, m 1 Oct 1851 by John T. St. Clair, minister.

Spencer T. Petty & Nancy West, m 9 Sept 1851 by John T. St. Clair, minister.

James Crow & Sally Workman, m 12 Oct 1851 by Manly Snipes, J. P.

Audner(?) Curl & Emma Johnson, m "within the last three months" by Levi Andrews, minister, 3 Nov 1851.

Jesse Glasson & Mary Brown, m "within the last three months" by Levi Andrews, minister, 3 Nov 1851.

Bird Gran & Mourning Thomas, m "within the last three months" by Levi Andrews, minister, 3 Nov 1851.

Caswell D. Wicker & Mary Utley, m 13 Nov 1851 by R. S. Marks.

Murphy Boyd & Mary Womack, m 20 Nov 1851 by R. S. Marks.

Samuel Gilmore & Delana Thomas, m 21 Dec 1851 by W. G. Harris, J. P.

James Pace & Elizabeth Hackney, m 26 Oct 1851 by Wm. Lineberry.

Andrew Headen & Martha L. Headen, m 11 Nov 1851 by Wm. Lineberry.

Pickney Ray & Margaret Burns, m 7 Dec 1851 by Wm. Lineberry.

Allen Young & Mary A. Williams, m 16 Dec 1851 by A. F. Olmsted, minister of St. Bartholomews Church, Pittsboro.

James P. Rosser & Isabella McArthur, m 31 Dec 1851 by W. G. Harris, J. P.

Joseph Dawson & Elizabeth Glasson, m 21 Dec 1851 by Manly Snipes, J. P.

John Jones & Elizabeth Burns, m 15 Nov 1851 by Jordan Tysor, J. P.

Allas Dawson & Nancy E. Richardson, m 2 Oct 1851 by A. Glasson, J. P.

Lucian B. Yaes & Parthena Upchurch, m 27 Dec 1851 by P. W. Dowd, minister.

Jacob Utley & Griza Jane Richardson, 1 Jan 1852 by Thoas Ragland, J. P. [this entry marked through]

James Hinsly & Prudence Mann, m 1 Jan 1851 by Thos Ragland, J. P.

Harbard Williams & Jane Sloan, m 1 Jan 1851 by Thos Ragland, J. P.

Calvin Green & Martha Barber, m 25 Sept 1851 by Johnson Olive, minister.

Avent Goodwin & Elizabeth Boling, m 1 Jan 1851 by Michael Thrailkill, J. P.

Nicholas Boling & Rebecca Holland, m 20 Nov 1851 by Michael Thrailkill, J. P.

H. C. Lashly & Susan Goodwin, m 12 Feb 1851 by M. Thrailkill, J. P.

Robert Burke & Patsey Fields, m 4 Jan 1851 by W. A. Rives(?), J. P.

Joseph Tysor & E. S. Tysor, m 1 Jan 1851 by Jordan Tysor, J. P.

Joseph Womble & Mary Jane Fox, m 9 Feb 1851 by A. S. Dowd, J. P.

John Phillips & Emily Welch, m 27 Aug 1851 by G. Lane, J. P.

Green Right & Mary Glasson, m 28 Sept 1851 by E. H. Straughan, J. P.

George A. Holt & Catharine Garner, m 20 Jan 1851 by Barzilla Mims, J. P.

Nathl Smith & Sally Hyde, m 29 Dec 1851 by A. J. Gilbert.

George W. Smith & Matilda Jolly, m 13 Jan 1852 by A. J. Gilbert.

Joseph Hilliard & Elizabeth Beal, m 4 Jan 1851 by A. Gaston Headen, J. P.

Anderson Olive of Wake County, & Emeline Esperann Florentine Yarborough of Chatham Co., m Thursday evening, 29 Jan 1852 by

Johnson Olive, minister.

Henry Lambert & Candice Phillips, m 1 Dec 1851 by Berry Jolly, J. P.

W. M. Hilliard & Jemima Clark, m 13 Jan 1852 by Berry Jolly, J. P.

Richard Rollins & Elenor Stuart, m 8 Jan 1852 by Thos Ragland, J. P.

Gilliam Carter & Martha Durham, m 12 Feb 1852 by Manly Snipes, J. P.

Samuel T. Culbertson & Jane Johnson, m 27 May 1852 by Wm. Lineberry, minister.

Stanford Way & Tempy Coble, m 31 Dec 1851 by S. G. Evans.

Oscar Harris & Agnes Peoples, m 25 March 1852 by _____, minister.

Isham Upchurch & Delia Beavers, m 23 Dec 1851 by E. P. Farrington, J. P.

Benjamin Smith & Mary Wilkie, m 11 Feb 1852 by A. J. Gilbert.

James M. Farrall & Matilda Stallings, m 13 May 1852 by Gaston Farrar.

James P. Holt & Terisa Holt, m 19 Feb 1852 by J. C. Wilson.

J. B. Lassater & Quinnetta Upchurch, m 15 Jan 1852 by G. W. Dowd.

John Rogers & Joanna Lutterloh, m 13 Jan 1852 by L. Burnett, minister.

Alexander Durham & Camelia Henderson, m 6 Apr 1852 by Richard Webster, J. P.

Lawrence J. Haughton & Martha Harris, m 2 March 1852 by A. F. Olmsted, minister of the Episcopal church.

William F. Croaker & Nelly Ann Archy, m 21 Dec 1852 by S. Stewart, J. P.

CHATHAM COUNTY NC MARRIAGES 1772-1868

Sam Thrift & Esperann Copeland, m 21 Dec 1852 by R. Webster, J. P.

John Wrenn & Julia Ann Bowen, m 17 Feb 1852 by A. S. Dowd, J. P.

Henry Jackson Watters & Elenor Morse(?), m 19 Feb 1852 by Samson Edwards, J. P.

Charles Willett & Amanda Lawhorn, m 18 March 1852 by C. Shields, J. P.

John Croker & Sarah Lineberry, m 21 Apr 1852 by S. Stewart, J. P.

Oliver McPherson & Malinda Lamb, m 29 Apr 1852 by Manly Snipes, J. P.

Howel Hearn & Jane Davis, m 12 May 1852 by R. Hatley, J. P.

Irvin Edwards & Priscilla White, m 16 May 1852 by Wm. P. Hadley, J. P. at the residence of Simon White.

William White & Delany Farrall, m 5 July 1852 by W. Hatch, J. P.

Henne Weber & Margarett Walker, m 18 July 1852 by A. F. Olmstead, minister of the Prot Episcopal Church.

William Bryant & Nancy Wilson, m 16 May 1852 by M. Thrailkill, J. P.

Andrew G. Williams & Martha Edwards, m 25 March 1852 by W. M. Rosson, J. P.

Nathan B. Bray & Catharine Edwards, m 8 June 1852 by Wm. M. Rosson, J. P.

Manliff Overman & Rebecca Benton, m 29 Aug 1852 by S. G. Evans.

Jno. A. Pugh & Mary L. Beal, m 21 Sept 1852 by G. E. Brown, minister.

Owen Evans & Martha Glass, 14 Sept 1852 by G. E. Brown, minister.

Adam Smith & Caroline Perry, m 12 May 1851 by O. McMath.

Wm. Johnson & Elizabeth Elmore, m 16 Nov 1851 by O. McMath, J. P.

Isaac Henderson & Susan McMath, m 5 Apr 1852 by O. McMath, J. P.

James Johnson & Martha Clark, m 15 Feb 1852 by O. McMath, bm.

Elisha A. Moore & Flora Jane Buchannon, m 16 Sept 1852 by R. S. Marks, J. P.

H. B. Marley & Emma E. Watson, m 8 June 1852 by Wm. Lineberry, minister.

W. S. McLean & Mary C. Marley, m 7 Sept 1852 by Wm. Lineberry, minister.

Robert H. Phillips & Mulbery(?) Jones, m 1 Apr 1852 by Berry Tally, J. P.

Allen Hullon & Margaret Hullen(?), m 4 Apr 1852 by Berry Tally, J. P.

Westly Barbor & Emeline Hatch, m 5 Aug 1852 by Berry Tally, J. P.

Calvin Fore & Rachel Dixon, m 17 Sept 1852 by S. Edwards, J. P.

Albert Hally & Nancy Mitchell, m 24 Oct 1852 by Thos Lambeth, J. P.

Wm Lassater, son of Thomas, & Martha C. May, m 29 Oct 1852 by R. Hally, J. P.

Horater Covet & Rinny Poe, m 10 Dec 1852 by Richard Webster, J. P.

Rhodes Pattishall & Martha Riddle, m 21 Dec 1852 by A. Sloan, J. P.

Wm Beal & Phebe Dowdy, m 27 Jan 1853 by A Gaston Heath(?), J. P.

Isaiah Fox & Polly Dorsett, m 10 Jan 1853 by A. Dallas Heube, J. P.

Jehu Boon & Sina Harman, m 30 Dec 1852 by Everett Fooshee, J. P.

Elisha Watson & Mary C. Rosson, m 13 Jan 1853 by A. M. Yarbor, J. P.

CHATHAM COUNTY NC MARRIAGES 1772-1868

Simms Upchurch & Talitha Williams, m 23 Dec 1852 by Johnson Olive, minister.

Elisha Womble & Kitty Crane, m 3 __ 1851 by E. Fooshee, J. P.

George B. Ellington & Prudence Wicker, m 26 Nov 1852 by T. Boling, minister.

Wm Martin & Louisa Thompson, m 9 Jan 1853 by A. Glosson, J. P.

George McBain & Julia Wright, m 21 Nov 1852 by A. Glosson, J. P.

Jno. M. White & Catharine Ray or Bay, m 16 Oct 1852 by Levi Andrews, minister.

James Cooper & Elizabeth Pennington, m 26 July 1853 by J. W. Hatch, J. P.

John Q. Smith & Rosanna Dorsett, 17 March 1853 by W. M. Rosson, J. P.

Alvis Harris & Susan Hadly, m 28 March 1853 by E. H. Straughan, J. P.

Joshua Discer & Elizabeth Loy, m 24 Oct 1852 by Wm. Loy, J. P.

Alexander McIver & Elizabeth Gilmer, m 14 July 1853 by A. Sloan, J. P.

Alias George & Eliza Ann Womble, m 20 Apr 1853 by G. E. Brown, minister.

Henderson Mulholland & Emily Powell, m 30 Dec 1852 by Thos Fowler, minister.

Duncan F. McIver & Minerva Headen, m 24 Aug 1853 by G. E. Brown, minister.

Edward Buckner & Martha E. Johnson, m 24 July 1853 by E. H. Straughn, J. P.

Jordan T. Johnson & Winny Ann Burns, m 20 May 1853 by W. G. Harris, J. P.

Henry Cox & Elizabeth Muckle, m 26 July 1853 by A. M. Yarboro, J. P.

James F. Jones & Emeline Edwards, m 1 March 1853 by W. M. Rosson, J. P.

Silas Mann & Nancy Mung(?), m 15 May 1853 by S. Mimms, J. P.

Mark Kelly & Emeline Ledbetter, m 5 Feb 1854 by Wm. G. Harris, J. P.

F. J. White & Margaret Pendergrass, m 12 Sept 1854 by W. G. Harris, J. P.

Calvin Watson & Nancy Kelly, m 11 March 1854 by W. G. Harris, J. P.

David Duncan & Jane Johnson, m 12 Feb 1854 by W. B. Carter, J. P.

James O. Gilleland & _____, m 12 Jan 1854 by W. M. Rosson, J. P.

Wm Segraves & Amanda Burns, m 23 Feb 1854 by Jordan Tysor, J. P.

James Lindly & Julia A. Stockan, m 16 Feb 1854 by W. P. Hadley, J. P.

Wm. Moore & Mary S. McCoy, m 18 Dec 1853 by J. O. Riggsbee, J. P.

Rufus H. Beavers & Louisa Lawter(?), m 2 Feb 1854 by C. B. Farrington, J. P.

John A. Aleboy & Emily Tysor, m 7 Dec 1853 by A. Gaston Headen, J. P.

Young Oldham & Mary T. Bennett, m 19 Apr 1853 by G. O. Riggsbee, J. P.

A. J. Walls & Lidda Miller, m 10 Feb 1854 by W. Loy, J. P.

Joseph Hooker & Mary J. Harris, m 19 Apr 1853 by A. F. Olmsted, minister.

David H. Rogers & Emily Faucette, m 22 Feb 1853 by A. F. Olmsted, minister.

J. W. Boon & Mary Lassater, m 8 Dec 1853 by A. L. Stough, minister.

John M. Brooks & Martha Welch, m 15 March 1854 by G. Lane, J. P.

J. W. Mann & Elizabeth Mitchum, m 20 Dec 1853 by R. Webster, J. P.

Charles Scott & Ann E. Yates, m 15 Dec 1853 by E. P. Farrington, J. P.

Isaiah M. Webster & Carolne Henderson, m 1 Dec 1853 by A. D. Headen, J. P.

Jasper Fooshee & Margaret Martin, m 1 Feb 1854 by W. P. Taylor, minister.

George W. Knight & Ruth C. Womble, m 20 Feb 1854 by R. T. Heflin, minister.

Richard Gunter & Nancy Penninton, m 12 Jan 1854 by J. W. Hatch, J. P.

Esley Hunt & Louisa Lutterloh, m 16 Dec 1853 by A. F. Olmstead, minister.

Wm Richardson & Marion Self, m 4 Dec 1853 by A. Glosson, J. P.

A. T. Wilson & Lina Stroud, m 27 Jan 1854 by R. F. Heflin, minister.

Wm Ward & Caroline Fields, m 19 Dec 1853 by H. B. Guthrie, J. P.

H. M. Rives & Dolly Byrd, m 22 Dec 1853 by J. C. Wilson, minister.

Canatha L. Whitfield & M. C. Brasington, m 8 Dec 1853 by John Hally, minister.

Stephen Braffon & Affa J. Hart, m 14 Feb 1854 by B. Tally, J. P.

James Cole & Polly Tillman, m 14 Feb 1853 by B. Tally, J. P.

Dennis Moffet & Ann E. Bray, m 23 March 1854 by G. Lane, J. P.

J. S. Hadney & Susan Brooks, m 22 Dec 1853 by W. Lineberry, minister.

John Clark & Sarah Davis, m 2 Feb 1854 by John Holt, minister.

W. J. Hunter & Martha Olive, m 4 Jan 1854 by J. C. Wilson, minister.

James C. Page & Emeline Fox, m 9 March 1854 by G. Lane, J. P.

Benjamin Crutchfield & Elizabeth Clark, m 14 Dec 1853 by G. W. Goldston, J. P.

N. B. Dunlap & Mary B. Emerson, m 10 Sept 1853 by A. J. Gilbert, minister.

Jos Holt & Nelly M. Murry, m 12 March 1854 by R. Hatly, J. P.

A. Kinloch & Mahala Glass, m 29 Dec 1853 by A. G. Headen, J. P.

John Williams & Ansse Ferrel, m 7 Dec 1853 by E. P. Farrington, J. P.

Hansel Ellis & Mary A. Riggsbee, m 1 Feb 1854 by J. W. Hatch, J. P.

L. B. Crewes & Nancy Hinson, m 30 Oct 1853 by A. D. Headen, J. P.

Frederick Yarboro & Elizabeth Dickson, m 9 March 1854 by A. M. Yarboro, J. P.

John D. Moore & Susan Walden, m 24 Dec 1854 by W. G. Harris, J. P.

David Caudle & Mary Brown, m 3 Dec 1854 by W. P. Taylor, minister.

Thos T. Phillips & Mrs. Mary Ann Poe, m 25 Dec 1854 by W. P. Taylor, minister.

Oran S. Poe & Frances Rives, m 25 Sept 1854 by R. T. Heflin, minister.

Edmond Phillips & Lovey Hilliard, m 11 Oct 1854 by Berry Tally, J. P.

John Way & Mary Ann Cledenan, m 24 Sept 1854 by S. G. Evans.

Mebane Coble & Paulina Browyers, m 8 Nov 1854 by S. G. Evans.

John Cox & Elizabeth Hackney, m 1 Oct 1854 by George Hinkman, J. P.

John Draton & Polly Siler, m 29 Oct 1854 by George Hinkman, J. P.

John M. Womble & Louisa Pattishall, m 11 Oct 1854 by Elias Bryan, J. P.

Eli Johnson & Elizabeth Burke, m 1 Nov 1854 by G. E. Brown, minister.

George W. Wilken & Dicy Ann Smith, m 24 May 1854 by A. Sloan, J. P.

John Loy & Eliza Stoner, m 2 July 1854 by W. Loy, J. P.

Josiah Tysor & Misouria Tally, m 14 Dec 1853 by Berry Tally, J. P.

Wm. R. Burgess & Isabella Yarborough, m 21 Nov 1854 by John Halley.

W. D. C. Riddle & Cynthia H. King, m 27 Sept 1854 by R. T. Heflin, V. D. M.

Hiram Vestal & Martha McPherson, m 12 Oct 1854 by W. B. Carter, J. P.

Robert E. Rives & Mary A. Brown, m 19 Aug 1855 by W. P. Taylor, minister.

J. J. Golston Jun. & Eliza Watson, m 14 Apr 1855 by W. P. Taylor, minister.

W. Womble & Mary Burke, m 28 March 1855 by W. P. Taylor, minister.

Wm Moran & Elmira McCoy, m 28 March 1855 by W. P. Taylor, minister.

Jos M. Siler & Sarah A. Low, m 4 Sept 1855 by W. B. Carter, J. P.

Wm. Tolleson & Malinda Allen, m 10 June 1855 by Samson Edmunds, J. P.

Alfred Peirce & Adaline Fox, m 6 Sept 1855 by W. B. Carter, J. P.

W. F. York & Emper Fox, 6 Sept 1855 by W. B. Carter, J. P.

Elwood Thompson & Alvira Hobson, m 25 March 1855 by S. Edwards, J. P.

Elisha Dean & Nelly Powers, m 24 March 1855 by C. Shields(?), J. P.

Johnathan Zackery & Martha Norwood, m 24 Feb 1855 by A. Glosson, J. P.

Henry Buckner & Elizabeth Crutchfield, m 12 Feb 1854 by S. Edwards, J. P.

W. Briles & Elizabeth Vestal, m 22 March 1855 by W. B. Cater, J. P.

Nathan Boon & Elizabeth Harman, m 10 Feb 1854 by J. W. Hatch, J. P.

Miller Burke & Martha A. Womble, m 16 Jan 1855 by W. Griffin, J. P.

Wm Brewer & Ann Malone, m 7 Apr 1855 by C. Shields, J. P.

Elijah Brown & Rebecca Caveny, m 5 Apr 1855 by C. Shields, J. P.

Johnathan Clark & Hammett Wilson, m 6 Apr 1853 by Eld Jesse Howel.

T. C. Dowd & Angelet Bray, m 22 Feb 1854 by A. S. Dowd, J. P.

Ben Webster & Joanna Elmer, m 9 March 1855 by O. McMath, J. P.

Stokes B. Edwards & Emeline G. Dowd, m 19 Nov 1854 by A. S. Dowd, J. P.

Aaron Emerson & Caroline Smith, m 26 Apr 1855 by C. Shields, J. P.

Josiah Forster & Malinda Staley, m 21 Apr 1855 by S. T. Culbreath, J. P.

M. Olive & Jane Upchurch, m 27 March 1855 by T. Boling, minister.

Sol J. Pickett & Beale McCoy, m 14 June 1855 by W. B. Carter, J. P.

Henry Powers & Mary Jackson, m 5 May 1855 by C. Shields, J. P.

Winship Petty & Eliza A. Clark, m 22 Nov 185 by J. Clark, J. P.

F. Richardson & Nancy Johnson, m 25 Nov 1854 by S. T. Culbreath, J. P.

M. Guthrie & Nancy Martin, m 12 May 1855 by A. Glosson, J. P.

Tarleton Johnson & Elizabeth Beal, m 14 June 1855 by G. W. Golston, J. P.

James Johnson & Sarah Hall, m 13 Aug 1855 by A. D. Headen, J. P.

Ruffin Jones & Anna Mimms, m 10 March 1855 by B. Mimms, J. P.

John W. Jones & Lilian Crutchfield, m 16 Nov 1854(?) by A. S. Dowd, J. P.

Wm Loy & Mary Boggs, m 23 Aug 1855 by O. Clark, J. P.

George F. Lindly & R. J. Crutchfield, m 6 Sept 1855 by S. T. Calburn, J. P.

Isaac H. Stroud & Mary E. Mann, m 12 Apr 1855 by Wilson Atwater(?), minister.

Elijah Alred & Elizabeth A. Fox, m 13 Apr 1854 by A. Edwards, J. P.

John Andrews & Piety Gean, m 25 Feb 1855 by A. Glosson, J. P.

John W. Beal & Rebecca Elkins, m 10 June 1855 by Berry Tally, J. P.

Aaron Beal & Apphia Johnson, m 28 Aug 1853 by H. B. Guthrie, J. P.

W. Cotten & Eliza Rollins, m 20 Feb 1855 by R. S. Macks, J. P.

Brooks Chick & L. K. Mashburn, m 18 Jan 1855 by B. Tally, J. P.

John W. Gilliam & Mary Sinclair, m 15 Feb 1855 by B. Tally, J. P.

John A. George & Elizabeth Henderson, m 18 Dec 1854 by G. E. Brown.

James Hathcock & Emily Elmore, m 6 May 1855 by A. D. Headen, J. P.

O. P. Hamlet & Happy Fooshee, m 11 Jan 1855 by E. P. Farrington, J. P.

Wm. M. Johnson & Mary E. Albright, m 8 May 1855 by A. W. Lineberry, minister.

Thomas Oldham & Sarah Joller, m 17 Apr 1855 by S. G. Brewer, J. P.

Negri McDanel & Sally Coggins, m 9 Aug 1855 by A. G. Gilbert, minister.

Wm. B. Moore & Elizabeth Mann, m 14 Aug 1855 by Geo W. Purify.

Manly Perry & Elizabeth McMath, m 3 Nov 1853 by A. H. Straughn, J. P.

Bazil Smith & Martha Ussey, m 5 Aug 1854 by C. C. Tally, J. P.

Seaborn Siler & Minerva Ellis, m 4 Sept 1855 by A. G. Gilbert, minister.

Alexander Smith & Sally Drake, m 21 Feb 1855 by R. S. Marks, J. P.

W. T. Sparrow & Anne Riggsbee, m 9 Oct 1855 by G. O. Riggsbee, J. P.

Wiley Tally & Jane Tillman, 5 March 1855 by C. C. Tally, J. P.

Andrew Wilson & Nancy Farrar, m 11 Feb 1855 by E. P. Farrington, J. P.

Alvin Ashworth & Lucy A. Hinesley, m 12 Oct 1857 by R. S. Marks, J. P.

Thomas Mitchell & Sarah Sauls, m 15 Sept 1856 by J. Clark, J. P.

Sydney Eubanks & Mary Horton, m 2 March 1852 by M. Thrailkill, J. P.

Nacy J. Neal & Susan Lasater, m 14 Sept 1856 by W. P. Taylor, minister.

CHATHAM COUNTY NC MARRIAGES 1772-1868

Thomas J. Lilly & Mary Ann Hatch, m 9 Sept 1856 by W. P. Taylor.

Luther Brown & Margaret Petty, m 25 Sept 1856 by W. P. Taylor.

William Hatch & Ann Neal, m 13 Oct 1856 by W. P. Taylor.

J. Massamore & Virginia Drake, m 22 Oct 1856 by W. P. Taylor.

Joseph T. Poe & Jane Clark, m 30 Nov 1856 by J. D. Brasington, J. P.

Oran Welch & Ruth N. Bray, m 25 Oct 1855 by G. Lane, J. P.

Thos C. Dixon & Sarah E. Albright, m 6 Jan 1853 by J. R. Holt, J. P.

Elisha Dismukes & Margaret Ray, m 31 Jan 1855 by H. A. London, J. P.

Basil M. Poe & Amelia A. Dismukes, m 14 Sept 1852 by L. Burnette, minister.

Seborne Ferrell & Polly Neal, m 7 Dec 1856 by J. W. Hatch, J. P.

John Foust & Alezernine(?) Snipes, m 7 Aug 1855 by A. W. Lineberry, minister.

Alfred Smith & C. C. Lutterloh, m 16 Feb 1853 by L. Burnett, minister.

Danl Murray & E. Smith, m 17 July 1856 by B. S. Mimms, J. P.

Martin Browning & Eliza Fooshee, m 4 Apr 1856 by G. E. Brown, minister.

James Gilbert & Mary Ellis, m 5 Nov 1856 by Atlas J. Gilbert.

Stephen Scott & Rachael Upchurch, m 28 Aug 1855 by Johnson Olive.

Nathl Moody & Rebecca C. Johnson, m 8 Nov 1856 by G. W. Gee, J. P.

Brantley Lambert & Martha Crutchfield, m 21 Sept 1856 by G. W. Gee.

CHATHAM COUNTY NC MARRIAGES 1772-1868

Bedford Solomon & Catharine Paschal, m 11 Sept 1856 by C. C. Tally, J. P.

N. R. Phillips & Jane Willet, m 12 Sept 1856 by C. C. Tally, J. P.

William Martin & Lydia Brewer, m 25 May 1856 by C. C. Tally, J. P.

Richard Ellis & Martha Goodwin, m 4 Nov 1856 by R. C. Council, J. P.

Wm. A. Humble & Elizth Smith, m 15 Sept 1856 by A. W. Lineberry.

Wm. C. Fields & A. M. White, m 25 July 1856 by A. G. Headen, J. P.

H. G. Foushee & Ann Headen, m 21 Sept 1856 by O. Churchill.

M. Lamb & Lydia J. Johnson, m 23 Apr 1856 by Gera Lane, J. P.

W. T. Sizemore & Louise McManus, m 30 Sept 1855 by C. Shields, J. P.

Allen W. Philips & M. A. Burrows, m 24 Nov 1855 by C. Shields, J. P.

Saml Johnson & Sally Jones, m 10 Jan 1856 by A. Glosson, J. P.

Wm. J. Hackney & Cathe Horton, m 7 Sept 1856 by J. H. Bynum, J. P.

Thos A. Edwards & Louisa M. Daniel, m 11 July 1856 by B. York.

H. O. Dunlap & Celia Headen, m 5 June 1856 by W. Lineberry.

Henry Oldham & Martha Stone, m 24 May 1856 by J. F. Rives.

James C. Fields & Phoebe A. Culberson, m 11 Oct 1855 by J. F. Rives, J. P.

Thos C. Willet & Mary Elkins, m 1 Oct 1855 by J. F. Rives, J. P.

Wm Ward & Avelissa Culberson, m 10 Aug 1855 by J. F. Rives.

John Manning & Louisa J. Hall, m 9 June 1856 by A. F. Olmsted.

John White & Nancy Lindley, m 10 Aug 1856 by A. M. Straughn, J. P.

John Goodwin & Lucy Ann Vick, m 23 Oct 1855 by H. J. Cotten, J. P.

Danl Vestal & Susan Brantley, m 19 Sept 1855 by N. B. Dunlap, J. P.

James Marshman & Sarah Tally, m 25 Apr 1856 by J. Patterson, J. P.

Thos Smith & Nancy A. Tally, m 6 Oct 1855 by C. C. Tally, J. P.

John P. Scotton & Lucinda Lane, m 1 Aug 1856 by W. B. Carter, J. P.

John Powers & Sabra Phillips, m 5 Apr 1856 by C. C. Tally, J. P.

Wm Elmore & Ferebee Stone, m 4 Jan 1856 by O. McMath, J. P.

David Jones & Sally Thomas, m 15 Oct 1855 by Levi Andrews, J. P.

John Dickson & Nancy McCoy, m 21 Dec 1855 by W. B. Carter, J. P.

Thos Dowdy & Elizth Crutchfield, m 17 Jan 1856 by A. S. Dowd, J. P.

J. W. Nall & Mary E. Moody, m 10 Jan 1856 by A. J. Gilbert, J. P.

Joshua Causey & Sarah Thompson, m 3 March 1856 by A. J. Gilbert, J. P.

Oliver Fogleman & Elizth Siler, m 9 March 1856 by A. W. Lineberry.

E. B. Kelly & Amie Tillman, m 2 Jan 1856 by C. C. Tally, J. P.

Robt Tally & Nancy Tally, m 2 Dec 1855 by C. C. Tally.

Madison Johnson & Phoebe Phillips, m 23 Dec 1855 by Minton Johnson.

James C. Thomas & Elizth Boon, m 30 Oct 1855 by W. G. Harriss.

Jesse G. McDaniel & Maranda Snipes, m 23 Nov 1855 by O. McMath.

James Gunter & Elizth Goodwin, m 23 Dec 1855 by Thos Ragland, J. P.

Calvin Jefferson & Mary Brafford, m 4 Dec 1856 by J. Patterson, J. P.

Joseph Pilkington & Malinda J. Pilkington, m 13 Apr 1856 by Lee Bynum, J. P.

Benjn. R. Avant & Francis Cross, m 18 Sept 1856 by R. S. Marks, J. P.

Jeremiah Tillman & Nancy Jane Womble, m 21 Aug 1856 by J. Patterson, J. P.

Thos Hinshaw & Elizth Evans, m 13 Nov 1855 by W. B. Carter, J. P.

Aaron Richardson & Elizabeth Hargrove, m 10 Feb 1856 by T. S. Culberson.

Aaron McPherson & Catharine Holliday, m 6 Apr 1856 by O. Clarke, J. P.

John Whitehead & Catharine McPherson, m __ Dec 1855 by O. Clarke, J. P.

Jesse Johnson & Tempe Stephens, m 23 Jan 1856 by O. Clarke, J. P.

Atlas J. Perry & Sarah Murray, m 27 Jan 1856 by O. Clarke, J. P.

Wm. J. Lambert & Nancy W. Fooshee, m 7 Feb 1856 by J. Jacks.

Murphy Williams & Emily Ausley, m 21 Feb 1856 by H. Council, J. P.

George Copeland & Elizabeth Meacham, m 15 March 1856 by R. Webster, J. P.

Yeargin Hart & Tabitha White, m 24 May 1856 by E. Fooshe, J. P.

Nicholas Covet & Elizabeth Poe, m 7 Dec 1855 by R. Webster, J. P.

A. J. Burns & Elizth Riddle, m 10 Aug 1856 by Minter Johnston.

James Farrar & Nancy Platt, m 25 Dec 1856 by Minter Johnston.

Isham Thrift & Salina Clark, m 30 Oct 1856 by R. Webster, J. P.

John Williams & Hasseltine Clarke, m 2 Oct 1856 by R. Webster, J. P.

John C. C. Kirkman & Elizabeth D. Stone, m 7 Aug 1856 by S. T. Culberson, J. P.

Thomas Lindley & Mary McMath, m 20 July 1856 by S. T. Culberson, J. P.

Joseph Dismukes & Elizabeth Lambert, m 15 Nov 1855 by J. C. Jackson, minister.

Joshua H. Hackney & Therissa Reece, m 3 Aug 1856 by J. C. Wilson, minister.

William Y. Farrell & Rebecca Bland, m 13 July 1856 by N. Melton, J. P.

Carizan Whit & Jane A. Crutchfield, m 3 Aug 1856 by E. H. Straughn, J. P.

William J. Hobby & Catharine Thrailkill, m 15 March 1856 by H. J. Cotten, J. P.

Ruffin Goodwin & Cynthia Boling, m 20 March 1856 by H. J. Cotten, J. P.

John McIver & Flora Ann McIver, m 4 Dec 1856 by Evander McNair.

James Ward & Cinthare Fields, m 29 March 1857 by James R. Reves, J. P.

Seban Derham & Elizabeth E. Man, m 30 Aug 1857 by L. Burnet, minister.

Solomon Brown & Jane Harman, m 7 Sept 1857 by W. Hanks, J. P.

M. M. Haughton & Mary A. Hinton, m 17 Feb 1857 by J. C. Wilson.

Barny May & Eliza C. Burns, m 14 Feb 1857 by S. G. Evins.

Wyatt Lawrence & Ruth McArthur, m 12 Feb 1857 by A. M. Yarbrough, J. P.

William Beaver & Nancy Jones, m 24 Dec 1856 by A. Gloson, J. P.

Jefferson Womack & _____, 4 Jan 1857 by B. S. Mims, J. P.

Henry M. Duke & Isabella Rives, m 24 Dec 1856 by S. G. Evins.

Aford Self & Mary Henderson, m 3 Aug 1857 by E. H. Straughn, J. r.

Joseph Johnson & Isabella Wright, m 9 Aug 1857 by E. H. Straughn, J. P.

Mac Dickens & Sally Gunter, m 4 Sept 1857 by Alex. Sloan, J. P.

Thos Martin & Martha Straughan, m 20 Dec 1855 by Wm Lineberry, minister.

William Dawson & Levena Vestal, m 7 Jan 1857 by Wm. Bailey, J. P.

James Fields & Mary Jones, m 13 Sept 1857 by Wm. Lineberry, minister.

William A. Perry & Rachel E. Teage, m 25 Aug 1857 by S. T. Culberson, J. P.

Durant Fogleman & Rachel Jane Record, m by W. B. Carter, J. P. "The date of the License was the 25th August 1857."

Lindly Thompson & Gulia Elma M. Kemp, m 12 July 1857 by S. Edwards.

John T. Womble & Rachael Stallings, m 12 Feb 1857 by John W. Tinen.

Basel Smith & Martha Leat, m 14 Jan 1857 by Berry Tally, J. P.

Jehu M. Perry & Margaret Teague, m 18 June 1857 by A. B. Headin, J. P.

A. T. Williams & Julia Wysor, m 13 Aug 1857 by John R. Holt, minister.

John Pearson & Eliza Heathcocok, m 6 Oct 1857 by Wm. P. Taylor, minister.

Chesley Ledbetter & Susan Brantly, m 29 July 1857 by Wm. P. Taylor, minister.

James Lane & Mahala P. Tyser, m 11 Oct 1857 by Joab H. Bray, J. P.

James Waddell & Mary C. Guthrie, m 20 Oct 1857 by Thomas C. Moss, minister.

Lasker B. Hicks & Lidia Purves, m 18 Aug 1857 by Joab H. Bray, J. P.

Pleasant Pendergrass & Mahalia Poe, m 18 Oct 1857 by N. Milton, J. P.

William Cooper & Margaret Hearn, m 13 Dec 1857 by N. Milton, J. P.

Samuel Thompson & Hesperan Perry, m 30 Dec 1857 by A. Glosson, J. P.

Younger D. Ray & Nany Thomas, m 15 Nov 1857 by A. Glosson, J. P.

Jonathan Zachry & Mary E. Norwood, m 17 Dec 1857 by A. Glosson, J. r.

Wilson Spivy & Cathrine Hughs, m 28 Oct 1857 by Elias Bryant, J. P.

Burwell Pleasants & Elizabeth Gunter, m 20 Aug 1857 by Thos Ragland, J. P.

Dempsey Lawrance & Nancy Davis, m 24 Oct 1857 by R. E. Studivent, J. P.

A. W. Yates & Hannah Lambert, m 22 Oct 1857 by G. W. Gee, J. P.

Harlee Beaver & Mary Cheak, m 15 Nov 1857 by W. J. Letterloh, J. P.

Manly Patishall & E. Howel, m 5 Jan 1858 by Henry J. Cotten, J. P.

Benjamin Parris & Elizabeth Beal, m 7 Feb 1858 by James F. Rives, J. P.

R. H. Taylor & Margarett M. Flass, m 22 Dec 1857 by James F. Rives, J. P.

William Phillips & Alpha T. Beal, m 28 Aug 1857 by Jas. F. Rives, J. P.

Hartin Ivy & Mary A. Andrews, m 24 Dec 1857 by Atlas Gilbert, J. P.

George W. Womble & Lydia Williams, m 21 Dec 1857 by Atlas J. Gilbert, J. P.

James F. Record & Racheal A. Fox, m 22 Dec 1857 by W. B. Carter, J. P.

Henry Spivy & Nancy Walker, m 24 Dec 1857 by A. M. Yarbrough, J. P.

John S. Jones & Martha Holt, m 30 Jan 1858 by B. S. Mims, J. P.

Eli Welch & Nancy Lambert, m 18 Dec 1858 by Jaob H. Bray, J. P.

Nathan Pike & Mariah Vestal, m 17 Dec 1857 by Daniel Worth, minister.

Jos. B. Cole & Mary Jane Herndon, m 12 Jan 1858 by John R. holt, minister.

Martin J. Smith & Elizabeth M. Wilkie, m 31 Dec 1857 by Isaac ____.

A. M. Johnson & Martha Womack, m 22 Dec 1857 by R. L. Mark(?), J. P.

Thos G. Andrew Hadly & Sarah P. Meyer, m 1 Oct 1857.

John E. Causy(?) & Mary E. Brewer, m 13 Feb 1858 by A. G. Headen, J. P.

William F. Ray & Sarah Pilkinton, m 5 Dec 1857 by R. Webster, J. P.

Carry C. Mann & Sarah G. Hackney, m 9 March 1855 by T. Bynum, J. P.

CHATHAM COUNTY NC MARRIAGES 1772-1860

Franklin Heathcock & Elizabeth Byans, m 28 Def 1857 by T. Bynum, J. P.

James D. Way & Annie Savnira Picket, m 14 Feb 1858 by D. Worth, minister.

Jonathan Braxton & Mary McPherson, m 11 Feb 1858 by Daniel Worth, minister.

Christian Fisk & Frances M. Mansfield, m 10 March 1858 by B. Faucett, J. P.

James K. Gibson & Matilda D. Bland, m 22 May 1857 by Robert Faucett, J. P.

J. W. Scott & Kate L. McLane, m 24 March 1858 by W. P. Taylor, minister.

V. A. T. Yates & Martha Harwood, m 22 Dec 1857 by S. Upchurch, J. P.

M. C. Leten & Kiddy Harwood, m 3 Feb 1858 by S. Upchurch, J. P.

Elbert Ausley & Sarah Goodwin, m 24 March 1858 by R. S. Marks, J. P.

Thomas W. Dowdy & Delia L. Clark, m 29 Apr 1858 by James F. Rives, J. P.

Bennet Upchurch & Sarah A. Lawrance, m 31 Jan 1858 by R. S. Marks, J. P.

Wesley Hackney & Fanny Whitaker, m 2 May 1858 by A. J. Riggsbee, J. P.

Luther Clegg & Flora A. Brooks, m 27 Apr 1858 by Revd. Robt P. Bibb, Methodist clergyman.

Thomas F. Williamson & Lydia M. Harris, m 11 May 1858 by W. P. Taylor.

T. J. Minter & Martha A. Gunter, m 6 May 1858 by Wm. P. Taylor, minister.

Willis R. Phillips & Delia Holt, m 15 Apr 1858 by Jos. A. Gilleland, J. P.

Jesse L. Smith & Eliza Adcock, m 19 March 1858 by Jos. A. Gilleland, J. P.

Moses R. Teague & Martha L. Marley, m 1 June 1858 by W. B. Carter, J. P.

N. C. Marley & Martha B. Jordan, m 2 June 1858 by W. B. Carter, J. P.

Elisha Hart & Mary Oldham, m 15 Dec 1858 by M. Bynum, J. P.

Henry L. Womble & Lucinda Holt, m 5 Aug 1858 by Thos Ragland, J. P.

John L. Hinton & Josephine Johnson, m 13 Aug 1858 by Johnson Olive.

Lewis M. Harward & Mary Jane Kirklin, m 27 May 1858 by Johnson Olive.

Andrew J. Moon & Mary E. Jones, m 18 July 1858 by O. Clarke, J. P.

Josiah Nigion & Mary W. Moon, m 22 Sept 1857 by O. Clark, J. P.

Nelson Light & Elizabeth Mason, m 20 May 1858 by O. Clark, J. P.

Andrew T. Riggsbee & Jane Durham, m 1 July 1858 by G. O. Riggsbe, J. P.

Joseph J. Moore & Mary R. Rives, m 27 Apr 1858 by G. E. Brown, minister.

John A. Gunter & Sarah J. Womack, m 12 Feb 1858 by W. G. Harris, J. P.

Caleb Johnson & Nany E. Racy, m 9 May 1858 by Richard Webster, J. P.

James C. Lash & Cathrine Ray, m 1 Aug 1858 by Richard Webster, J. P.

Jefferson B. Mansfield & Ann G. Gean, m 8 Sept 1858 by William P. Taylor, minister.

Joseph Segrove & Elizabeth Burns, m 26 Aug 1858 by Minter Johnson.

Sidney Witherspoon & Frances Lasater, m 31 July 1858 by J. C. Wilson.

William Browning & Martha Smith, m 26 Aug 1858 by Elias Bryan, J. P.

Alfred Horton & Cornelia Lewis, m 13 June 1858 by A. Glosson, J. P.

Alfred Brown & Emily B. Guthrie, m 1 Sept 1858 by J. C. Thomas.

Wiley J. Boon & Ann Moore, m 23 Sept 1858 by John W. Hatch, J. P.

John Bland & Matilda Boon, m 11 Oct 1858 by J. W. Hatch, J. P.

J. W. Chadwick & Mary A. Harman, m 14 Oct 1858 by W. P. Taylor.

Gadis Copeland & Elizabeth Dismukes, 23 Dec 1857 by Lucian Burnett, minister.

Taylor Man & Martha Mann, m 20 OCt 1858 by Lucian Benton, minister.

James Welch & Winny Deaton, 26 Aug 1858 by Chesley Jones, J. P.

Wm A. Edwards & Sarah Jane Teague, m 5 Sept 1858 by Wm. Lineberry, minister.

Wm Saunders & Elizabeth Wright, m 5 Oct 1858 by N. Milton, J. P.

Joseph Myrick & Abi Glosson, m 23 Sept 1858 by Levi Andrews, minister.

Alfred Nevells & Patte Morgan, m 19 Oct 1858 by Wilson Atwater, minister.

Green Brewer & Delana N. Marthal, m 25 Nov 1858 by J. W. Tinen, minister.

Allen Shilds & Nancy Tally, m 27 Apr 1858 by A. Buroghs, J. P.

William M. Burns & Margaret J. Clegg, m 8 Dec 1858 by W. G. Harris, J. P.

Isaac Simons & Janie Gilmore, m 8 Oct 1858 by W. T. Harris, J. P.

Enoch Clark & Winy A. Gunter, m 21 Dec 1858 by J. W. Tinnen, minister.

Henry Boon & Margaret Straughan, m 16 Dec 1858 by J. W. Hatch, J. P.

Robert Johnson & Louisa Kearn, m 22 Dec 1858 by J. W. Hatch, J. P.

E. M. Neal & Julia Bryant, m 8 Dec 1857 by Wm. Griffin, J. P.

B. R. Ward & Margaret Foushee, m 3 Nov 1858 by Wm. Griffin, J. P.

Atta Pendergrass & Martha Neal, m 30 Dec 1858 by J. W. Tinny, minister.

John R. Patishall & Frances Dickens, m 6 Jan 1859 by A. Sloan, J. P.

B. Holland & A. Jenckens, m 30 Dec 1859 by J. W. Willins, minister.

Daniel Jackson & Elizabeth B. Jeffers, m 3 Jan 1859 by W. A. Rives, J. P.

William Williams & Hesperan Bullard, m 27 Jan 1859 by J. Williams, J. P.

William Haywood & A. C. Burns, 8 Feb 1859 by F. A. London, J. P.

John W. Page & Margaret Ramsey, m 4 Dec 1857 by N. Collin Hughes.

S. B. Simmons & Ann M. London, m 9 Feb 1859 by N. Collin Hughes.

William Haywood & Ann E. Burns, m 8 Feb 1859 by H. A. London, J. P.

A. R. Burgess & Adeline Record, m 24 Aug 1858 by W. B. Carter, J. P.

Isaac T. Brooks & Margaret E. Rives, m 8 Feb 1859 by S. Tillett.

David V. Ferguson & _____, m 10 Oct 1858 by W. B. Carter, J. P.

J. H. Farrow & Elizabeth Avant, m 25 Aug 1858 by W. S. Chaffin, minister.

A. C. Council & Louvena Upchurch, m 23 Dec 1856 by Johnson Olive.

Roderick Goodwin & Elizabeth Goodwin, m 15 Jan 1859 by R. E. Sturdivant, J. P.

Joshua Causey & Jane Culberson, m 12 Sept 1858 by Atlas J. Gilbert.

R. Buckhannon & Vicy Gilmore, m 14 Nov 1858 by Alex Sloan, J. P.

William V. Hodgins, & Cathrine Coble, m 17 Dec 1857 by Wm. Zackary J. P.

A. R. Burges & Jane Record, m 25 Sept 1858 by W. B. Carter, J. P.

Thomas Hensy & Nancy Forrester, m 25 Jan 1859 by Atlas J. Gilbert, J. P.

Jonathan E. Mashborn & Lucinda Smith, m 18 Nov 1858 by J. A. Scott, J. P.

Randolph Turlington & Emeline Utley, m 11 Jan 1859 by Thos Ragland, J. P.

Thomas Philips & Eliza Neal, m 3 Feb 1859 by Atlas T. Gilbert, J. P.

John R. Bright & Nancy Womble, m 26 Jan 1850 by Atlas T. Gilbert, J. P.

Henry Branson & Mary Deaton, m 23 Dec 1858 by Chesley Jones, J. P.

Allen Shields & Nicy Tally, m 27 Apr 1858 by Z. A. Brooughs, J. P.

Edwin Teague & Lucy Young, m 14 Nov 1858 by Wm. Yarbrough, J. P.

Henderson Upchurch & Dealan Williams, m 27 Jan 1859 by Johnson Olive.

William Thompson & Margaret Stone, m 14 Nov 1858 by Wm. Zachary, J. P.

J. H. Farrow & Elizabeth Avant, m 25 Aug 1858 by W. S. Chaffin, minister.

C. B. Clegg & Martha E. S. Stroud, m 7 Dec 1856 by Solomon Lea.

P. J. Pervis & Lidia Mashburn, m 6 Feb 1859 by J. A. Scott, J. P.

Robert A. Beal & _____ Moody, m 19 Dec 1858 by James T. Rives, J. P.

Levi Copeland & Elizabeth Hashal, m 23 Jan 1859 by J. W. Hatch, J. P.

Nathan Steward & Susanna Stagg, m 7 Nov 1858 by O. Clark, J. P.

James M. Upchurch & Isabel Thomas, m 18 Jan 1859 by A. M. Yarbrough, J. P.

C. P. Luther & Sallie J. Emerson, m 16 March 18 59 by Y. S. Yarbrough.

Solomon Boggs & Temperance GLenn, m 17 Sept 1858 by Wm. Loy, J. P.

Gideon Copeland & Elizabeth DIsmukes, m 23 Dec 1857 by L. Burnett, minister.

William A. Mansfield & Louisa M. Buchhannon, 17 Nov 1858 by R. Faucett, J. P.

Christopher Teague & Louisa A. York, m 18 Nov 1858 by Wm. Loy, J. P.

James P. Roper & Jane McArthur, m 15 Dec 1858 by A. M. Yarbrough, J. P.

Hilliard S. Buckhanan & Emeline Adeline Laromer, m 1 Dec 1858 by A. M. Yarbrough, J. P.

Moses H. Roach & Edah McPherson, m 26 Dec 1858 by Oliver Clark, J. P.

William Bowden & Nany A. Allen, m 30 Dec 1858 by Oliver Clark, J. P.

Manly Lane & Julia Siler, m 27 Feb 1859 by Wm. Lineberry, minister.

Sherod Morgan & Mary Straughan, m 27 Feb 1859 by Wm. G. Harris, J. P.

Edward Powel & Perlina Riggsbee, m 24 Feb 1859 by G. W. Fooshee, J. P.

James A. P. Williams & Oranna B. Crumpton, m 23 Nov 1858 by G. E. Brown.

Spencer Murry & Nancy Johnson, m 19 March 1859 by J. S. Lasater, J. P.

Michael Stein & Emma Plat, m 30 Dec 1858 by Minter Johnson.

Uel Pendergrass & Amanda Marks, m 23 March 1859 by W. G. Harris, J. P.

Reddin Jenkins & Mary Holt, m 3 May 1859 by M. J. Ramsey, J. P.

J. M. Riggsbee & Elizabeth Oldham, m 31 March 1859 by Jas. F. Mason, Baptist minister.

William Fooshee & Jeana Burke, m 27 Apr 1859 by J. S. Yarbro.

James Henderson & Mary M. Perry, m 20 MArch 1858 by O. McMath, J. P.

James Lindley & Hannah Andrew, m 23 Nov 1859 by O. McMath, J. P.

George Phillips & Ruth Sanders, m 4 Aug 1859 by J. Patterson, J. P.

William Carter & Phoebe Brown, m 8 May 1859 by John Hinshaw, minister.

CHATHAM COUNTY NC MARRIAGES 1772-1868

Alvis Nelson & Hannah C. Fogleman, m 24 Apr 1859 by John Hinshaw, minister.

R. D. Poe & Delia Johnson, m 3 Apr 1859 by John W. Hatch.

W. A. Taylor & Cora Long, m 28 June 1859 by L. Burnett.

A. J. Goldston & Catherine Rives, m 24 Nov 1858 by A. H. Headen.

Samuel P. Teague & Sally M. Edwards, m 18 Jan 1859 by Wm Lineberry, minister.

Wm. S. Edwards & Eliza E. Martin, m 7 Nov 1858 by Wm Lineberry, minister.

Thos Q. Mimms & Claura Holt, m 10 July 1859 by Elias Bryant, J. P.

Arnal Turner & Susan Dosett, m 5 June 1859 by William Lineberry, minister.

Basil Hearn & Haratt Webster, m 22 May 1859 by William Lineberry, minister.

John Y. Gunter & Emeline Copland, m 31 July 1859 by J. Tillet, minister.

John A. Fogleman & Sarah E. Liles, m 7 Aug 1859 by J. M. Stout Esqr.

Henry M. Lineberry & Mary A. White, m 30 July 1859 by John Hinshaw, minister.

Owen L. Johnson & Pamelia F. Arrington, m 21 July 1859 by Minton Johnson.

James McDaniel & Mary Johnson, m 31 May 1859 by Minter Johnson.

George W. Poe & Emily M. Gilmore, m 21 July 1859 by Alex. Sloan, J. P.

Addison Lineberry & Martha K. Duncan, m 23 Dec 1858 by E. K. Straughan, J. P.

John White & John Allen [sic], m 30 March 1859 by Oliver Clark, J. P.

Goodman Stagg & Jane Allen, m 23 May 1859 by Oliver Clark, J. P.

C. M. Poe & Amanda J. Farell, m 7 Aug 1859 by J. W. Hatch, J. P.

Marcus Womble & Hesperan Drake, m 7 Apr 1859 by R. E. Sturdivant, J. P.

John Elkins & Rebecca Smith, m 8 June 1859 by J. Patterson, J. P.

James Washington Bird & Edner Hatwood, m 7 Oct 1859 by O. Clark, J. P.

Henry Edwards & Sally Larrup, m 10 Nov 1859 by Oliver Clark, J. P.

Alvis Bright & Mary Cooper, m 8 Aug 1859 by G. W. Hatch, J. P.

Daniel Hinshaw & Cinthia Caroline Nation, m 17 Aug 1859 by John Hinshaw, minister.

William Thomas & Elizabeth Yarbrough, m 22 Aug 1859 by A. M. Yarbrough, J. P.

Samuel Richardson & Caroline Jane Rawnsly, m _____ 1859 by Nathaniel Norwood.

B. N. Smith & Julia E. M. Britt(?), m 9 Nov 1859 by John Hinshaw, minister.

Riffin Workman & Martha Morgan, m 10 Oct 1858 by John S. Stroud, J. P.

C. C. Swayze & Susan Hill, m 9 Nov 1859 by Moller Hughs.

Richard B. Holt & Maryan Johnson, m 25 Oct 1859 by B. S. Mims, J. P.

John Pike & Mary Ann Fogleman, m 28 Apr 1859 by Alfred Isley.

Irvin Nall & Nancy Woody, m 4 Dec 1859 by D. F. McIver, J. P.

Timothy J. Moody & Elizabeth Campbell, m 24 March 1858 by N. B. Dunlap, J. P.

David Williamson & Martha Brewer, m 7 June 1858 by C. C. Tally, J. P.

William S. Hilliard & Martha J. Shields, m 14 March 1858 by C. C. Tally, J. P.

Calvin L. Council & Isley A. Wilson, m 14 Dec 1859 by R. C. Council, J. P.

Mathew Lindsey & Martha Beall, m 13 Nov 1859 by Y. Oldham, J. P.

George Done & Adeline Bridges, m 3 July 1859 by Z. A. Boroughs.

Benjamin Roberts & Ann Culberson, m 11 Nov 1859 by Z. A. Boroughs, J. P.

Newton Stout & Sarah E. Andrew, m 29 Dec 1859 by Oliver McMath, J. P.

Robert Goodwin & Caroline Bynum, m 12 Dec 1859 by R. C. Council, J. P.

Henry Gilleland & Martha Craven, m 25 Oct 1859 by Joab Bray, J. P.

Leander Kivett & Susanah Forrester, m 27 March 1859 by Joab H. Bray, J. P.

William Goodwin & Rebecca A. Council, m 22 Dec 1859 by R. C. Council, J. P.

Spencer Hicks & Sophia Hicks, m 13 Nov 1859 by Joab H. Bray, J. P.

T. W. Cheak & Elizabeth E. Lane, m 12 Oct 1859 by Joab H. Bray, J. P.

Richard Riddle & Mary A. Marks, m 13 Jan 1860 by H. Burke, J. P.

Calvin Mitchel & Nancy Wright, both free persons of color, m 18 Jan 1860 by Jas W. Wh---.

John A. Jones & Peggy Lasater, m 12 Jan 1860 by W. Lineberry, minister.

Alfred Hadley & Mary C. Copper, m 22 Sept 1859 by Samson Edwards, J. P.

Richard A. Jones & Elizabeth Cheak, m 1 Jan 1860 by Atlas J. Gilbert.

Richard B. Webster & Velania Utly, m 25 Jan 1860 by A. M. Yarbrough, J. P.

James P. Keaton & Mary A. Kelly, m 18 Dec 1859 by A. M. Yarbrough.

Chesley Jones & Elizabeth B. Hatch, m 5 Feb 1860 by J. Patterson, J. P.

Joseph J. White & Lenora J. Bright, m 14 Aug 1859 by Geo. Hickman, J. P.

Edward Harris & A. E. Guthrie, m 24 Jan 1860 by G. E. Brwon.

Gabriel Drake & Martha Burke, m 18 Jan 1860 by R. E. Sturdivant, J. P.

William A. Mitchel & Martha A. Goodwin, m 8 Feb 1850 by R. E. Sturdivant, J. P.

Thomas J. Clegg & Eliza McIver, m 28 Feb 1860 by G. A. Russell.

Agner G. Hacks & Martha A. Lambeth, m 21 Feb 1860 by John Tillett.

Joshua T. Cheak & Frances Camel, m 27 Nov 1859 by Levi Andrews.

Carmillin M. Bane & Frances Wright, m 19 Jan 1860 by Levi Andrews.

J. P. Johnson & Temperance Mann, m 12 Jan 1860 by Robt Lane, J. P.

Newton White & Sarah Thomas, m 24 Aug 1856 by Robt Lane, J. P.

Wm. K. Pettey & Martha J. Lindley, m 19 Dec 1859 by Richard Webster, J. P.

Joel Stinard & Eliza Smith, m 14 March 1860 by R. C. Council.

William C. Council & Caroline Wynn, m 20 June 1859 by R. C. Council, J. P.

Alexander McDaniel & Letha R. Carter, m 28 Aug 1859 by Thos A. Brooks, J. P.

W. G. Stockard & Emily A. Albright, m 15 Sept 1859.

Phillip W. Hasken & Harriett A. Platt, m 6 Oct 1859 Minter Johnson.

Thomas Campbell & Nancy Henderson, m 26 July 1859 by Richard Webster, J. P.

R. C. Gregory & Julie Alston, m 3 Oct 1859 by L. K. Willen, M. G.

A. F. Phillips and Mary Womble, m 14 Sept 1859 by Atlas J. Gilbert.

Sion Mitchel & Elizabeth Drake, m 29 Sept 1859 by R. E. Sturdivant, J. P.

William Wortham & Ann Galfin, m 2 Feb 1859 by J. O. Wilson.

James Burges & Rebecca J. Williams, m 20 July 1859 by W. W. Harper, J. P.

Samuel Richardson & Louisa Williams, m 22 Feb 1860 by O. Clark, J. P.

Thoams Jones & Martha Mann, m 14 Nov 1859 by B. L. Mims, J. P.

James May & Rachel Andrews, m 15 Jan 1860 by Oliver Clark, J. P.

Allen Petty & Jane Richardson, m 13 Oct 1859 by A. Glosson, J. P.

J. C. Riggins & Caroline U. Council, m 8 March 1860 by O. Churchill.

Richard R. Moore & Sarah A. Headin, m 16 March 1860 by Thos yarbro.

Joseph W. Emerson & Phebee A. Powers, m 5 March 1860 by D. F. McIver, J. P.

Elias Fields & Rebecca N. Beal, m 22 Dec 1859 by D. F. Mciver, J. P.

Henry Moody & Lucy Bright, m 8 Jan 1860 by D. F. McIver, J. P.

William S. Gunter & Mary J. L. Holt, m 10 June 1860 by J. W. Wellons.

James P. Taylor & Virginia M. Hanks, m 12 June 1860 by John N. Tiner, minister.

J. T. Taylor & A. H. Alston, m 10 Apr 1860 by W. P. Taylor, minister.

John Q. Headin & Mary E. Brown, m 22 Apr 1860 by J. W. Wheeler, Elder in church.

Micajah Castleberry & Elizabeth Miller, m 3 Aug 1860 by R. Faucett, J. P.

Cornelius Edwards & Martha Thrift, m 18 Aug 1850 by Young Tilham, J. P.

Vinton Hart & Sally Oldham, m 31 Sept 1860 by J. W. Willon.

A. J. Harrington & Lucy A. Womack, m 13 Dec 1859 by R. S. Marks, J. P.

William Oldham & Mary Malone, m 10 Sept 1860 by J. W. Willons.

J. D. Hackney & Jemima Garner, m 25 March 1860 by J. C. D. Brasington, J. P.

Wm. F. Jones & Sarah E. Crutchfield, m 20 May 1860 by R. Lambert, J. P.

William H. Morris & Esperan Moore, m 5 April 1860 by Robt. Faucett, J. P.

Henry T. Moore & Eliza C. Straughan, m 25 Sept 1860 by Wm. Lineberry, minister.

Zah Pattishall & Adelina Knight, m 3 May 1860 by W. G. Harris, J. P.

Barzalla Hinshaw & Laura C. Elke(?), m 21 Feb 1860 by John Hinshaw, minister.

Levi B. Williams & Mary A. Lindley, m 4 Sept 1860 by E. H. Straughan, J. P.

John M. Stout & Lotty Rives, m 14 June 1860 by D. F. McIver, J. P.

Zachariah H. Morgan & Elizabeth Rives, m 12 July 1860 by D. F. McIver, J. P.

Carney Mims & Aluyrd Rollins, m 19 Sept 1859 by R. S. Marks, J. P.

Elisha Pepkins & Polly Cass, m 6 Oct 1859 by R. S. Marks, J. P.

Wm. M. Wicker & Mary Mann, m 24 June 1860 by R. Faucett, J. P.

Hezekiah Gross & Hannah B. Burns, m 1 Oct 1860 by J. A. McDonald, J. P.

Bratton A. Sanders & Bethana Copeland, m 5 Apr 1860 by J. W. Hatch, J. P.

Jacob Kaly & Elizabeth Conaby, m 15 May 1860 by Minter Johnson.

L. C. Lineberry & Elizabeth A. Hanna, m 28 Oct 1859 by Minter Johnson.

John M. Gunter & Elizabeth Jones, m 28 June 1860 by Minter Johnson.

Quilla Johnson & Tabitha Bishop, m 8 March 1860 by Joseph D. Brasington, J. P.

Samuel Perry & Nancy Lewis, m 8 March 1860 by Levi Andrews.

Dan Abernathy & Mary E. Sloan, m 24 Apr 1860 by A. M. Yarbrough, J. P.

W. B. Carter & Mary Dark, [no date] m by E. H. Straughan, J. P.

Willey Smith & Martha Jane Tally, m 14 Sept 1860 by C. C. Tally, J. P.

Nathan Clark & Mary Powers, m 18 Sept 1860 by M. Bynum, J. P.

William L. Myrick & Milly Jones, m 4 Aug 1859 by Chesley Jones, J. P.

William H. Brown & Catherine Malone, m 2 Feb 1860 by A. McIntire, J. P.

Alvin Barber & Sarah Elkins, m 61 Nov 1858 by A. McIntire, J. P.

Oran Stokes & Bethany F. Martindale, m 12 July 1860 by J. A. Scott, J. P.

Alexander Jenkins & Affiat Doud, m 22 Dec 1857 by A. McIntire, J. P.

Mannual Oldham & Rachel M. Burke, m 28 Aug 1857 by A. McIntire, J. P.

Hezekiah Dowdy & Sarah Gilmore, m 9 Jan 1858 by A. McPeter, J. P.

Almond Ausley & Sarah Matthews, m 25 March 1860 by Alex Sloan, J. P.

John T. Kelly & Sarah B. Gunter, m 15 Nov 1860 by J. W. Tiner, minister.

R. S. Powel & Mary L. Garrett, m 8 Nov 1860 by Wm. H. Jordan Jr.

Levi W. Kimball & Eliza A. Moon, m 4 Oct 1860 by H. A. Durham, J. P.

W. A. Fox & Mry Kirby, m 16 July 1860 by T. Bynum.

Thos B. White & Nancy Jones, m 11 Oct 1860 by Atlas J. Gilbert.

Solomon F. Hugens & Mary C. Prescott, m 16i Sept 1860 by J. M. Stout, J. P.

John Phillips & Amey Brewer, m 14 Jan 1860 by Z. A. Boroughs, J. P.

Josiah Mann & Mariah Martindale, m by 25 Oct 1860 by Z. A. Boroughs, J. P.

Alexander Hobby & Lucy Goodman, m 28 Oct 1860 by R. C. Council, J. P.

John E. Mason & Priscilla True, m 28 Oct 1860 by J. J. Riggsbee, J. P.

James G. Watson & Sarah N. Bynum, m 14 Nov 1860 by J. F. Elitt, M. .E. Church South.

James Keild & Catharine Jones, m 29 March 1860 by Z. A. Boroughs, J. P.

Wm. L. Pope & Sarah L. T. Bagly, m 20 Dec 1860 by O. Churchill.

Benjamin Kivey & Matilda Spivy, m 15 Oct 1860 by Elias Bryan, J. P.

Basel E. Webster & Sarah A. Straughan, m 30 Oct 1860 by Wm. Lineberry, minister.

Richard Webster & Mary A. Shillings, m 30 Oct 1860 by Wm. Lineberry, minister.

James C. Dowd & Henrietta M. Rives, m 3 Oct 1860 by A. J. Emerson, M. G.

Green Philips & Susan Beal, m 16 Dec 1860 by G. W. Emerson, J. P.

Mathias McCollom & Adeline Kirby, m __ Sept 1860 by J. P. Mason, Bapt. minister.

Thomas R. Morrer & Annie Sears, m 12 Dec 1860 by J. W. Tinen, minister.

Thomas C. Cox & Cora Jane Gunter, m 9 Jan 1861 by J. W. Tinen, minister.

Joseph Kelly & Elizabeth Spivy, m 20 Dec 1860 by J. N. Clegg, J. P.

Henry S. Martin & Ellen Reeves, m 24 Dec 1860 by Wm. Lindley, J. P.

Benjamin Spivy & Malinda Yarbrough, m 15 Oct 1860 by Elias Bryan, J. P.

Wyatt P. Rawlins & Eliza Jane Smith, m 20 Feb 1860 by J. W. Wellons.

Edward J. Hale & Mariah R. Hill, m 15 Jan 1861 by Robt B. Sutton, Record of St. Bartholomews Church, Pittsboro.

Algenon Horton & Eliza Wheeler, m 17 Feb 1861 by R. C. Council, J. P.

James A. Baker & Mary Churchill, m 11 March 1861 by R. C. Council, J. P.

William Harman & Margarett Johnson, m 12 Feb 1861 by G. E. Brown.

F. M. Straughan & Eliza Masingale, m 23 Dec 1860 by K. E. Sturdivant.

Daniel Tilman & Salinah Burges, m 12 March 1861 by R. E. Sturdivant.

Albert J. Holt & Abba Davis, m 5 March 1861 by R. E. Sturdivant, J. P.

John McIver & Cathrine Wicker, m 14 March 1861 by John A. McDonald, J. P.

Robert Carpenter & Angeline Cotton, m 20 Dec 1860 by R. S. Marks.

J. M. Lindley & F. F. Glen, m 21 Feb 1861 by J. M. Stout, J. P.

Owen Coltrane & Mary Jane Hinshaw, m 17 March 1861 by J. M. Stout.

Edwin D. Patterson & Louisa M. Siler, m 5 Feb 1861 by J. Carny, Elder.

Joshua Clark & Lucy Hart, m 8 Sept 1860 by Jordan Tyner, J. P.

David C. Brown & Sarah Oldham, m 13 Oct 1859 by J. C. Hooker, J. P.

W. B. Cole & Nancy Johnson, 27 Sept 1860 by Minter Johnson.

Thomas Waddell & Emily C. Tyner, m 27 Sept 1860 by Minter Johnson.

D. W. Coggins & Hannah Cheak, m 6 Jan 1861 by J. C. Hooker, J. P.

John R. Horton & Sarah A. Fooshee, m 18 Feb 1861 by J. C. Burke Esqr.

Joseph Pendergrass & Lutitia Marks, m 24 Dec 1860 by John S. McClenahan, J. P.

P. N. Fooshee & Mary A. Upchurch, m 16 Feb 1861 by O. Churchill.

Mark Smith & Samantha Cook, m 12 Dec 1860 by John S. McClenahan.

Thomas G. Jones & Henrietta Russel, m 20 May 1860 by S. Glosson, J. P.

Robert D. Hackny & Malinda Copeland, m 14 Feb 1861 by J. W. Watson, J. P.

William F. Lasater & Harriett Robertson, m 15 Jan 1861 by S. Gilmore.

James Poe & Milchiel Gilmore, m 1 Feb 1860 by S. Gilmore.

R. M. Jones & May L. Burns, m 14 Feb 1861 by S. Gilmore.

Mahon Loy & Harriett Stuart, m 15 Nov 1860 by H. O. Durham, J. P.

Maben G. Clark & Julia A. Russell, m 30 Dec 1860 by H. O. Durham, J. P.

Peter Allen & Emely Stuart, m 22 Jan 1861 by H. O. Durham.

Geo. W. Bowden & Esperan Roper, m 26 Nov 1860 by Robt Lambert, J. P.

Henry Thomas Vestal & Sunnett Climy, m 25 Dec 1860 by Robt Lambert, J. P.

James Coggin & Tenessee Tally, m 12 March 1861 by Z. A. Boroughs, J. P.

Henry M. Loyd & Elizabeth Pattishall, m 7 March 1858 by Stephen Gilmore.

Alfred Hadly & Cathrine Cheak, m 15 Nov 1860 by Levi Andrews.

Sugar Jones & Susan Scott, m 30 Dec 1860 by Z. A. Boroughs, J. P.

Wm. Harris & Elizabeth Elkins, m 14 Dec 1860 by Z. A. Boroughs, J. P.

Riley Cagle & Nancy Dove, m 24 Dec 1860 by Z. A. Boroughs, J. P.

William F. Headen & Mary D. Goldston, m 7 Jan 1861 by S. D. Adams.

J. H. Dark & J. E. Henderson, m 17 Apr 1861 by E. H. Straughan, J. P.

Julius Blalock & Martha Beal, m 16 Apr 1861 by G. W. Emerson, J. P.

W. F. Stroud & L. H. Hunter, m 18 Apr 1861 by S. D. Adams

Edward McKinon & Elizabeth Wicker, m 12 Apr 1860 by Thomas Quigley, Catholic Priest of Raleigh, N. C.

Alvan Hearn & Easther Davis, m 18 March 1861 by R. E. Sturdivant, J. P.

Samuel Thomas & Ann E. Russel, m 23 Dec 1860 by Levi Andrews.

Thomas N. Hill & E. E. Hall, m 4 June 1861 by R. B. Sulton, Rector of St. Bartholomews Church, Pittsboro.

Hall Horton & Adaline King, m 31 May 1861 by Joseph D. Brasington, J. P.

Wm. F. Riggsbee & Celia A. Mitchel, 19 May 1861 by A. J. Riggsbee, J. P.

Brantly M. Ray & Nancy J. Paxton, m 9 June 1861 by A. J. Riggsbee, J. P.

Thomas M. Brown & Nancy J. Fooshee, m 5 May 1861 by John S. McClenahan.

William J. Hasler(?) & Mary D. Goldston, m 7 May 1861 by S. D. Adams. [This entire entry stricken]

Nathaniel Foster & Rhoda E. Jordan, m 5 May 1861 by Jos. A. Gilleland, J. P.

Abner Brannon & Selanee Deaton, m 27 March 1861 by Chesley Jones, J. P.

Stephen Johnson & Catharine Lineberry, m 11 Apr 1861 by William Loy, J. P.

Alfred Stuart & Claranda Jane Evins, m 30 Apr 1861 by James W. Jones.

Martin M. Fogleman & Elizabeth Cooper, m 24 Feb 1861 by D. L. Staly, J. P.

Manly Buckner & Rebecca Jones, m 14 Dec 1860 by Levi Andrews.

Jesse J. Buckner & Martha M. Romley, m 20 Apr 1861 by J. M. Stout, J. P.

John D. Dickens & Camma Cooper, m 14 Apr 1861 by D. L. Staly, J. P.

William A. Duman & Bethena P. Bridges, m 1 May 1861 by Wm. Lineberry, minister.

Thomas Johnson & Caroline Williams, m 5 March 1861 by O. Churchill.

Benjamin M. Beal & Sarah B. Johnson, m 17 June 1861 by W. G. Harris, J. P.

William B. Lett & Sarah Penington, m 3 July 1861 by H. H. Burke, J. P.

Benjamine R. Bryan & Emeline A. Alston, m 11 Sept 1860 by G. E. Brown, minister.

Merritt Upchurch & Annie Mann, m 2 June 1861 by R. Faucett, J. P.

Henry A. Mann & Martha McMath, m 24 June 1861 by James Hutton, J. P.

Chesley E. Page & Julia A. Bray, m 31 May 1861 by Robert Lambert, J. P.

CHATHAM COUNTY NC MARRIAGES 1772-1868

Thomas Buckner & Fanny Glover, m 3 Sept 1861 by Wm. Lineberry, minister.

W. E. Ellington & A. F. Cammel, m 20 Aug 1861 by Levi Andrews.

B. G. Lambert & Elizabeth Bynum, m 14 Aug 1861 by W. P. Taylor, minister.

Thomas Camel & Sarah Stone, m 15 Sept 1861 by E. H. Straughn, J. P.

William Zachary & Marand McDaniel, m 25 Aug 1861 by S. D. Adams.

Robert W. Waddell & Elizabeth Ann Dorsett, m 27 Aug 1861 by S. D. Adams.

Glover Avent & Caroline A. Partridge, m 18 oct 1861 by A. M. Ylarbrough.

F. A. Mann & F. M. Borwn, m 4 Oct 1861 by L. Burnett, minister.

Joseph B. Johnson & Catha Ann Lasater, m 7 July 1861 by O. Churchil, minister.

William H. Darke & Sallie H. Harris, m 3 Oct 1861 by H. W. Peoples, J. P.

William Hackney & Sarah Fitts, m 23 Oct 1861 by Robert Lambert.

Thomas Emerson & Martha Jane Hutton, m 23 nov 1860 by D. F. McIver, J. P.

Timothy B. Burke & Elizabeth A. Mansfield, m 10 March 1861 by D. F. McIver, J. P.

John McIntyre & Mary A. Campbell, m 24 Dec 1861 by D. F. McIver, J. P.

John Moffit & Mariah Louisa Farrell, m 18 Dec 1861 by John W. Hatch, J. P.

J. H. Harwood & H. M. Mason, m 9 Jan 1862 by J. J. Riggsbee, J. P.

CHATHAM COUNTY NC MARRIAGES 1772-1868

Edward W. Atwater & Margarett A. Bynum, m 5 Dec 1861 by L. Burnett, minister.

Madison Perry & Sarah Johnson, m 27 Oct 1861 by O. Clarke, J. P.

John S. McLenahan & M. S. Alston, m 29 Oct 186 1 by S. D. Adams, minister.

Murdoc Black & Nellie McLane, m 8 Dec 1861 by O. K. Caldwell, minister.

William Lassater & Eliza Riggsbee, m 28 May 1861 by R. E. Sturdivant, J. P.

John Elmore & Mary A. Cruchfield, m 2 Jan 1862 by O. McMath, J. P.

Wesley Smith & Nancy Henderson, m 18 Aug 1861 by John S. McClenahan, J. P.

John M. Emberson & M. Yarbrough, m 22 Feb 1861 by Atlas J. Gilbert, J. P.

Ruffin Goodwin & Mary A. Bolding, m 5 Feb 1862 by O. Churchill, minister.

Thomas Goodwin & Martha An Carmicle, m 16 Jan 1862 by R. C. Council, J. P.

C. M. Snipes & Margarett E. Lamb, m 4 Feb 1862 by Samuel Baldwin, minister.

W. H. Fogleman & Elizabeth J. Ferguson, m 18 Dec 1861 by J. M. Stout, J. P.

Thos C. Rosser & Mary C. Ragland, m 9 Jan 1862 by A. M. Yarbrough, J. P.

Alexander Jinkins & Lidia Woble, m 5 May 1861 by Atlas J. Gilbert.

Orren Andrews & Rosanah Dowd, m 11 Apr 1861 by Atlas J. Gilbert, J. P.

Albert Parin & Sarah Ellis, m 30 Jan 1862 by R. C. Council, J. P.

CHATHAM COUNTY NC MARRIAGES 1772-1868

James Ray & Cornelia Andrews, m 31 Oct 1861 by A. J. Gilbert.

Wm. T. Dowdy & Elizab Straughn, m 2 Jan 1862 by M. Bynum, J. P.

Burwell W. Brown & Sarah H. Cross, m 28 Feb 1862 by R. S. Marks, J. P.

Atlas J. Headen & Eliza White, m 16 Feb 1862 by Richard K. Moore, minister.

Nathan Rogers & Elizabeth Harris, m 11 Feb 1862 by Nathaniel Norwood, minister.

Wm. J. Siler & Mary Holmes, m 11 July 1861 by D. S. Staly, J. P.

James P. Shaw & Nancy Albright, m 25 July 1861 by M. O. Durham, J. P.

Carney C. Atwater & Amelia Baldwin, m 6i March 1862 by L. Burnett, minister.

Pinkney Thrift & Sarah Tripp, m 26 Feb 1862 by G. W. Foushee, J. P.

James E. Perry & Frances C. Johnson, m 17 Dec 1861 by E. H. Straughn, J. P.

Thomas C. Council & Susanah Stone, m 19 Dec 1861 by R. C. Council, J. P.

Wm. H. Hill & Lucy J. Rives, m 26 Aug 1861 by R. Dorsett, J. P.

Wm. A. Burges & Francis Brasington, m 27 Aug 1862 by Joseph P. Brasington, J. P.

Mathew Dowdy & Nancy Sanders, m 14 Setp 1862 by A. McIntyre, J. P.

Silas J. Douglas & Elizabeth Douglas, m 25 Sept 1862 by A. M. Yarbrough, J. P.

John McDonal & Adaline Johnson, m 13 Feb 1862 by James. F. Rives, J. P.

James N. Gee & Martha A. Adcock, m 5 June 1862 by Richard r. Moore, minister.

CHATHAM COUNTY NC MARRIAGES 1772-1868

Hawkins Riggsbee & Catharine Sparrow, m 22 March 1862 by J. J. Riggsbee, J. P.

Johnson Clarke & Elizabeth E. Harman, m 12 June 1862 by S. D. Adams, minister.

James Thomas & Catharine Dixon, m 4 May 1862 by H. O. Durham, J. P.

J. B. Bell & Elizabeth F. Mason, m 4 Sept 1862 by J. C. Wilson.

John B. Kelly & Marget Rives, m 13 June 1862 by C. W. Andrews, minister.

Isaac Lawhorn & Elizabeth Willet, m 27 March 1862 by C. D. Shields, J. P.

James Stone & Nancy Buckner, m 18 Feb 1862 by J. M. Stout, J. P.

James Jones & Margarett Mathews, m 17 June 1862 by R. E. Strudvaint, J. P.

Blakely Hart & Elizabeth Ross, m 31 March 1862 by James F. Rives, J. P.

C. B. Denison & Mag M. Cowen, m 4 Jan 1863 by Robt B. Sutton, Rector of St. Batholomew Church, Pittsborough.

Joseph Daniel & Chiney Gardner, m 30 Dec 1862 by R. C. Council, J. P.

Alvis Brown & Louisa Foushee, m 4 Dec 1862 by H. W. Peoples, J. P.

M. L. Trask & Sarah R. Pitman, m 25 Dec 1862 by J. F. Smott.

Murdoc Street & Mary Jane Siler, m 24 Dec 1862 by Richard B. Moore.

William Baldwin & Mary J. Stroud, m 9 Dec 1862 by Wilson Atwater, J. P.

Lewis Desern & Annah J. Brown, m 12 Jan 1863 by Ab. J. Ramsey, J. P.

Samuel Brewer & M. E. Johnson, m 25 Dec 1862 by A. J. Riggsbee, J. P.

John Bouroughs & Decimus T. Holmes, m 17 March 1864 by W. P. Taylor

Nathan Dixon & C. J. Glenn, m 5 Sept 1862 by H. O. Durham.

William Hinley & Mary Dixon, m 13 Jan 1863 by H. O. Durham, J. P.

John Pennington & Elizabeth Mitchell, m 29 Nov 1863 by J. D. Brasington, J. P.

Richard Pilkington & Mary Lewis, m 23 May 1863 by John S. Stroud, J. P.

Elbert Windham & Nancy Buckhanan, m 30 Aug 1863 by John W. Scott, J. P.

Harrison Walls & Emily Britton, m 5 July 1863 by John W. Scott, J. P.

C. C. Williams & Susana Allred, m 28 Jan 1863 by J. W. Stout.

William Allen & Peggy Bowden, m 30 Nov 1861 by O. Clark, J. P.

Lewis A. Apple & Sarah A. Ellett, m 24 Feb 1862 by J. M. Stout, J. P.

Wm Bryant & ELizabeth Craton, m 22 Apr 1862 by H. H. Buck, J. P.

Gilliam Carter & Mary Ann Durham, m 5 Apr 18623 by R. Webster.

Robert Webster & M. C. Riggsbee, m 26 Sept 1863 by E. T. Hackney.

Patrick Evans & Frances Gee, m 19 May 1863 by James B. Long, J. P.

William Johnson & Nancy Cheek, m 22 May 1862 by R. Dorsett, J. P.

Wm. Moore Jr. & Sallie Jane Thomas, m 24 Dec 1864 by John W. Scott, J. P.

Josiah Davis & Adelne Peter, m 23 Oct 1862 by Oliver Clark, J. P.

W. H. Fogleman & Elizabeth Ferguson, m 1 Sept 1863 by W. H. Bobbit, minister.

Rev. Wm Lineberry & Mary A. Webster, m 5 Apr 1864 by C. H. Straughn, J. P.

Rev. J. B. Martin & Clara Scarborough, m 25 Dec 1863 by W. H. Bobbit, minister.

S. G. Norwood & Martha Ann Hackney, m 23 Oct 1863 by George Kirkman.

J. W. Petty & Mary T. Poe, 18 Sept 1863 by Minter Johnson, minister.

A. H. Sloan & M. J. Neal, m 10 Sept 1863 by Wm. Gunter, J. P.

George Tilman & Nancy Cheek, m __ Nov 1863 by A. J. Tillet, J. P.

David Williams & Mary M. Bryant, m 14 Jan 1864 by J. D. Brasington.

John Gowins & Jane Gowins, m 13 Nov.1862 by A. McIntyre, J. P.

Sims Pendergrass & Virginia Williamson, m 19 July 1863 by J. C. Burke, J. P.

Isaac Bright & Seni J. Martin, m 16 Apr 1863 by Wm. Gunter, J. P.

Robert Cheek & Mary Beal, m 29 Nov 1863 by R. C. Cotton, J. P.

William Williams & Cleopatra Cheek, m 24 Nov 1861(?) by O. Clark, J. P.

S. F. Baldwin & Julia F. Bynum, m 1 Sept 1862 by E. P. Fearington, J. P.

John E. Allen & Sarah M. Stout, m 16 Jan 1863 by Samuel Pearce, minister.

Nathan Hillard & Bettie Elkins, m 29 Nov 1863 by R. C. Cotton, J. P.

James P. Johnson & Sarah Gean, m 26 Dec 1860 by Minter Johnson, minister.

Levi Rodgers & Julia Burke, m 10 Apr 1862 by 19 Apr 1864 by Thos A. Brooks, J. P.

P. G. Snowdon & A. C. Loudon, m 11 Nov 1863 by Robt B. Sutton, minister.

James P. Campbell & Fannie Hutson, m 29 Dec 1863 by A. J. Emerson, minister.

Robert T. D. Foushee & Mary Fitts, m 17 Jan 1864 by A. J. Emerson, minister.

B. F. Shaw & A. H. Marsh, m 26 Jan 1864 by A. J. Emerson, minister.

Joseph Dixon & Rebecca Vestal, m 20 March 1864 by H. O. Durham, J. P.

Thos W. Farrish & Cornelia Harris, m 17 Jan 1864 by A. J. Emerson, minister.

William Johnson & Margarett Johnson, m 20 June 1864 by J. R. Brasington, J. P.

Green Clark & Cornelia Elmore, m 5 May 1864 by E. C. Straughn, J. P.

Wm. F. Harlle & C. C. McRae, m 23 June 1864 by J. D. Brasington, J. P.

William Pike & Maria Teague, m 2 March 1864 by J. W. Scott, J. P.

John Range & Pettie Oldham, m 29 May 1864 by J. C. Hooker, J. P.

E. Jones & Francis Hatch, m 6 Apr 1864 by Chesley Jones.

Obed Farrar & Ann Clegg, m __ May 1864 by J. B. Martin, minister.

S. M. Holt & Eugenia Bland, m 22 Jan 1864 by J. W. Hatch, J. P.

Jasper Rogers & Mary Self, m 27 March 1864 by R. Dorsett, J. P.

John J. Knight & Sarah J. Ellington, m 25 May 1864 by J. B. Martin, minister.

John Farrell & Mary Holt, m 22 July 1864 by J. W. Hatch.

Henry Robertson & Biddie Riggsbee, m 23 July 1863 by G. W. Fooshee, J. P.

Barb Munholland & Adaline Kelly, m 19 Feb 1862 by E. D. Farrington.

John W. Atwater & C. J. Fearington, m 15 Apr 1861 by E. F. Fearington, J. P.

Madison Davis & Elizabeth C. Long, m 27 Dec 1860 by James B. Long, minister.

Thomas N. Marshall & Caroline Falkner, m 2 May 1864 by H. O. Durham, J. P.

W. H. McGee & Demaris Jenkins, m 3 Nov 1859 by E. P. Fearington.

Harman Sears & H. Williams, m 20 Dec 1860 by E. P. Fearginton.

John Griffin & Ellen McDaniel, m 10 March 1865 by M. Johnson, minister.

Lemuel Ellis & Tacitia Hatly, m 11 Dec 1863 by Dempsy Johnson, J. P.

Herman Coble & Pheby Nelson, m 27 July 1865 by John Hinshaw, minister.

F. S. Davis & M. J. Brewster, m 15 Oct 1864 by Robt B. Sutton, minister.

John Hammock & S. Yarborough, m 7 June 1865 by J. H. Hatch, J. P.

John Hamock & Elizabeth Holder, m 18 Sept 1865 by John S. Ferrell, J. P.

'Jesse Petty & C. Rosser, m 27 Dec 1864 by T. C. Moses, minister.

CHATHAM COUNTY NC MARRIAGES 1772-1868

A. J. Bare & Sallie Crutchfield, m 29 March 1865 by Wm Lineberry, minister.

Jos Rosser & Hannah Gross, m 22 Aug 1865 by J. T. Rives, J. P.

R. S. Webb & S. Clegg, m 21 Dec 1865 by W. H. Bobbit, minister.

John J. Siler & Margaret J. Rosser, m 13 Nov 1865 by W. S. Edwards, J. P.

Alexander Way & Lidia Hinshaw, m 14 May 1865 by John Hawkins, minister.

John Buma & Sally Malone, m 16 Oct 1862 by A. W. McIntyre, J. P.

A. Vestal & Lorena Bass, m 19 Nov 1865 by W. S. Edwards, J. P.

Samuel Pennington & Mary Womble, m 8 Oct 1864 by J. D. Brasington.

B. J. M. Hughs & Mary A. Lane, m 7 Dec 1865 by E. H. McManus, J. P.

J. F. Kemp & Mary A. Pike, m 17 Feb 1865 by J. M. Stout, J. P.

William Duncan & Susan Moran, m 3 Sept 1864 by J. M. Stone, J. P.

S. H. Dowdy & Nancy J. Straughn, m 19 May 1864 D. C. Murchison, J. P.

D. C. Murkerson & Lydia A. Smith, m 2 June 1863 by Atlas J. Gilbert, J. P.

W. J. Mims & M. J. Gunter, m 28 June 1863 by E. Bryan, J. P.

William Johnson & Sallie E. Andrews, m 17 Aug 1863 by Atlas J. Gilbert, J. P.

Thomas Andrew & Mary Henry, m 30 Nov 1860 by Atlas J. Gilbert, J. P.

Thomas Mathis & Sally Patterson, m 24 MArch 1863 by Atlas J. Gilbert, J. P.

Wm. B. Farrar & Martha D. Watson, m 27 Jan 1864 by Gaston Farrar, minister.

Thos Brady & Vetra Drake, m 28 Oct 1863 by John W. Scott, J. P.

Nathaniel Forrister & Amanda Jones, m 8 Oct 1863 by Rev. R. R. Moore.

Rev. N. McKay & Miss Annie B. S. Pettigrew, m 14 May 1863 in the ___ of Haywood, by C. K. Caldwell, minister.

W. S. Webster & Joseph Ann Adcock, m 9 Oct 1864 by C. C. Tally, J. P.

Tarlton Johnson & Eliza Ann Burk, m 20 Dec 1864 by Atlas J. Gilbert.

D. L. Stedman & Mary Brewer, m 13 Sept 1864 by Elias Bryan, J. P.

Charles Dowde & Ester Ann Williams, m 19 May 1864 by D. C. Murchison, J. P.

Alexander Caucy & Sarah George, m 4 Sept 1864 by C. C. Tally, J. P.

Enoch Williams & Sarah Ivy, m 26 Oct 1864 by George W. Fooshee, J. P.

Oliver H. Cooper & Julia E. Fox, m 18 Sept 1864 by Jos A. Gilleland, J. P.

John M. Campbell & Permelia F. Burne, m 26 Oct 1864 by W. H. Bobbit.

George W. Vinson & Sarah Williams, m 11 March 1864 by O. Clark, J. P.

W. L. London & M. C. Haughton, m 14 Nov 1864 by Robt B. Hutton, Rector of St. Bartholomews Church, Pittsboro.

Henry Hatch & Eliza Tillman, m 18 Sept 1864 by Atlas J. Gilbert, J. P.

Wesley Upchurch & Sarah Ann Goodwin, m 6 OCt 1864 by James B. Long, J. P.

James Henderson & Affiah Camel, m 21 July 1864 by L. Burnett.

CHATHAM COUNTY NC MARRIAGES 1772-1868

James Bass & D. Morgan, m 27 June 1863 by ___ Baldwin, minister.

Thomas Beal & Darke Willet, m 27 Dec 1864 by Atlas J. Gilbert, J. P.

N. K(?). Smith & Emily J. Shields, m 14 July 1864 by C. C. Tally, J. P.

Richard Evans & Betsy Largh, m 3 Oct 1864 by James B. Long, J. P.

John Staly & Tryphena Fox, m 13 Nov 1864 by L. A. Hutson, minister.

Simeon Lowery & Julia Richardson, m 19 Apr 1864 by L. Burnett, minister.

Jos Monroe & M. McKally, m 8 __ 1864 by T. C. Moses, minister.

Thos A. Lawrence & Kizy Holt, m 21 Dec 1864 by S. H. Gibson, J. P.

O. M. Dosett & Fanny McIntyre, m 24 Sept 1865 by James F. Rives, J. P.

Samuel M. Moran & Sarah E. Whitehead, m 26 March 1865.

William Barbee & Ady Cotton(?), m 17 Jan 1865 by O. Church, minister.

Benjamin Gunter & Elizabeth J. Neal, m 21 Oct 1865 by C. A. Boon, minister.

John Phillips & M. A. Phillips, m 12 March 1865 by G. W. Emerson, J. P.

Joseph Cox & Margaret Hackney, m 4 Sept 1865 by Wm. Lineberry, minister.

John Z. Foushee & M. E. Nalls, m 29 Jan 1865 by G. W. Emerson, J. P.

Wm. Caudle & Tabitha Hatch, m 22 Jan 1865 by J. D. Brasington, J. P.

James M. Ward & Rachael McDaniel, m 1 Sept 1865 by H. O. Church, J. P.

Fuller Webster & Affia Smith, m 7 Sept 1865 by C. Justice, J. P.

James G. Snead & Mary Ann Miller, m 6 Dec 1864 by C. A. Boon, minister.

C. C. Williams & Julia C. Andrew, m 23 Aug 1865 by William Griffin, J. P.

John H. Dafford & A. A. Campbell, m 17 Dec 1865 by C. Justice, J. P.

John Baringer & Mary W. Bland, m 27 Oct 1866 by J. W. Gibson, j. P.

J. T. Wates & A. E. McIver, m 15 Oct 1865 by T. W. Guthrie, minister.

James Martindill & Nancy Ellis, m 1 Oct 1865 by E. H. McMorris(?), J. P.

Benjamin Harris & Caroline Campbell, m 20 Dec 1863 by E. H. Straughn, J. P.

Winship Oldham & Mary Griffin, m 14 June 1864 by A. McIntyre, J. P.

A. R. Johnson & Janna Hackney, m 4 Sept 1865 by Wm. Griffin, J. P.

V. R. May & Sarah J. Hadly, m 3 Sept 1864 by H. H. Gibbons, minister.

T. J. Morris & Mary A. Robertson, m 28 Sept 1865 by Wm. Griffin, J. P.

Sidney J. Tally & Henrietta Murchison, m 21 Dec 1865 by Atlas J. Gilbert, J. P.

Wm. G. Brewer & Mariah Phillips, m 2 Apr 1865 by Atlas J. Gilbert, J. P.

W. C. Cruchfield & M. Rives, m 18 Dec 1865 by A. M. Self, J. P.

Nell Norwood & Mary M. Johnson, m 3 Dec 1865 by W. B. Carter, J. P.

M. F. Emerson & Mary Etta Headen, m 22 Oct 1865 by A. J. Emerson, minister.

Johnathan Jobe & Abigal Hickman, m 16 Dec 1865 by H. O. Durham.

A. J. Tilman & Mary Ann Hatch, m 7 Sept 1865 by Atlas J. Gilbert.

Alfred Ellis & Rebecca Stone, m 19 Dec 1865 by W. A. Long, J. P.

J. K. Knight & Margarett A. Sloan, m 24 Dec 1865 by G. P. Moore, J. P.

Richard Whitehead & Martha Albright, m 24 Dec 1865 by James Griffin, J. P.

Loami Hatley & Harriet Council, m 5 Oct 1865 by William Griffin, J. P.

Arthur Whitehead & Margarett Culberson, m 15 Jan 1865 by J. M. Stout, J. P.

Lemuel Ellis & Salitha Hatley, m 11 Dec 1865 by Dempsy Johnson, J. P.

John A. Partin & Fanny Dodd, m 8 Nov 1865 by W. A. Long, J. P.

William Stone & Yoma Hatley, m 12 Jan 1865 by H. Council, J. P.

J. B. McClenahan & M. E. Ellington, m 29 Aug 1865 by Samuel Baldwin, minister.

M. G. Elmore & Mary Perry, m 6 June 1865 by Richard Webster, J. P.

Young Jones & Willie Holt, m 27 Dec 1865 by J. K. Gibson, J. P.

Dr. John R. Hogan & M. A. Goldston, m 6 Dec 1865 by James Phillips, J. P.

Winship Nall & Ann Thomason, m 20 Oct 1865 by H. O. Dunlap, J. P.

Andrew Ferguson & Lovina Hobson, m 3 Dec 1865 by W. S. Edwards, J. P.

H. W. Johnson & Margarett M. Teague, m 7 Dec 1865 by W. S. Edwards, J. P.

B. B. Phillips & Margarett L. Womble, m 19 Oct 1865 by Atlas J. Gilbert, J. P.

Hiram Bland & Tempy Griffin, m 15 Nov 1865 by William Griffin, J. P.

Jacob Marshall & Margaret Nelson, m 27 Sept 1865 by W. B. Carter, J. P.

Kilbee Hodgen & Julia A. Pickett, m 25 Jan 1866 by John Hinshaw, minister.

W. H. H. Richardson & Pyrana M. Mobly, m 4 Aug 1866 by O. Clarke, J. P.

G. W. Wilcox & J. C. Palmer, m 31 Jan 1866 by R. A. Willis, minister.

Edward Parish & Ofalia Kelly, m 26 Jan 1866 by P. Mason, minister.

A. G. Snipes & Sarah Barbee, m 10 Jan 1866 by N. A. Long, J. P.

C. M. Stedman & Kate De Wright, m 8 July 1866 by Robt B. Sutton, Rector of St. Batholomews, Pittsboro.

W. S. Griffin & Sina J. Bright, m 15 Jan 1866 by Wm. Griffin, J. P.

Thos V. Hinson & Mary Mirack, m 18 Jan 1866 by Atlas J. Gilbert, J. P.

W. R. Pattishall & Semantha Johnson, m 8 Jan 1866 by M. Johnson, minister.

Robert Wilson & Mahala McManis, m 25 Feb 1866 by E. H. McManis, J. P.

Wm. Henderson & Sarah Self, m 30 Jan 1866 by A. M. Self, J. P.

Thomas Clarke & Mary J. Thomas, m 25 March 1866 by J. C. Justice, J. P.

E. A. Moffit & M. F. Hatch, m 18 Jan 1866 by J. N. Farrell, minister.

John Burnett & Caroline Stroud, m 21 Jan 1866 by Samuel Baldwin, minister.

Roberson Thomason & Francis Teague, m 28 Jan 1866 by H. O. Durham, J. P.

Columbus Johnson & Della Wright, m 16 Jan 1866 by Wm Lineberry, minister.

Jos Boggs & Emaine Moore, m 14 March 1866 by Wm Lineberry, minister.

Wm H. Ellis & Mary E. Bray, m 14 Jan 1866 by E. H. McManis, J. P.

Pleasant Gillum & Emma Harris, m 18 Feb 1866 by O. Clark, J. P.

Sidney Ivy & Emily Andrews, m 26 Jan 1866 by William Griffin, J. P.

Wm. H. Brooks & Saphrona A. P. Myrack, m 19 Oct 1865 by Atlas J. Gilbert, J. P.

Robt Shields & Martha J. Harden, m 27 Feb 1866 by E. H. McManis, J. P.

James Boroughs & Bella Cole, m 9 Jan 1866 by A. J. Emerson, J. P.

Robert Burns & Cornelia Burns, m 16i Aug 1866 by J. N. Farrell, minister.

Marion Perry & M. F. Harman, m 25 Jan 1866 by H. H. Gibbons, minister.

Alvis Riddle & Emily Bullard, m 19 Feb 1866 by O. S. Poe, J. P.

A. G. Hearn & E. Hathcock, m 18 Feb 1866 by W. P. Taylor, minister.

Atlas Neal & Susan Williamson, m 17 Feb 1866 by Wm. Griffin, J. P.

O. M. Lutterloh & Caroline Henderson, m 15 March 1866 by C. Justice, J. P.

Hezekiah Teag & Lovey Burk, m 17 March 1866 by W. Y. Edwards, J. P.

A. W. Palmer & V. Ranes, m 31 June 1866 by A. N. Turner, minister.

Arther Ellmoor & Silvia Foust, m 7 July 1866 by H. O. Durham, J. P.

John Micher & Martha Johnson, m 10 Feb 1866 by S. B. Perry, J. P.

F. M. Moore & L. J. Wright, m 21 March 1866 by Robt B. Sutton, Rector of St. Bartholomews Church.

John W. Lea & Celia Dismukes, m 9 Aug 1866 by Rev. John F. Burnett.

Wm Tripp & Emily Thrift, m 1 Apr 1866 by J. B. Farrar, minister.

Neill Kidd & Polly Branson, m 28 March 1866 by E. H. McManis, J. P.

Samuel Johnson & Tamar Southerlan [stricken]

E. P. Stinson & Callie E. Brooks, 17 May ___ by Atlas J. Gilbert, J. P.

Jessee Campbell & A. Self, m 28 March 1866 by C. Justice, J. P.

J. T. Brooks & Sallie E. Brooks, m 4 March 1866 by Elias Bryan, J. P.

Jos A. Johnson & Annie Gilmore, m 2 Aug 1866 by J. A. McDonal, J. P.

N. A. Gilmore & Mary A. Pattishall, m 21 Aug 1866 by J. A. McDonal, J. P.

Wm. A. Kelly & Martha J. Webster, m 13 June 1866 by E. Bryan, J. P.

Wm. R. Mitchell & Mrs. M. J. Riggsbee, 13 Sept 1866 by M. T. Baldwin, J. P.

James M. Thomas & Caroline Perry, m 20 June 1866 by O. Clark, J. P.

H. H. Burk & Mrs. A. E. Johnson, m 1 Aug 1866 by R. H. Marsh, minister.

Robt M. Burns & M. S. Johnson, m 19 Feb 1866 by Minter Johnson, minister.

Cargle Which & S. A. Crutchfield, m 19 July 1866 by O. Clark, J. P.

Atlas G. Phillips & Parthenia A. Tally, m 16 Jan 1866 by A. J. Gilbert, J. P.

Gillim Carter & Mrs. M. E. West, m 7 Aug 1866 by C. Justice, J. P.

Ruffin Holt & P. E. E. Mann, m 13 Aug 1866 by J. N. Farrell, minister.

Henry Petty & Adaline Williams, 6 Sept 1866 by O. P. Hamlett, J. P.

H. Lambert & E. R. Dorsett, m 9 Sept 1866 by Jos A. Gilleland, J. P.

Henry M. Coble & Elizabeth M. Yorke, m 1 Sept 1866 by John Hinshaw, minister.

A. J. Loyd & Francis Williams, m 2 Sept 1866 by W. C. Thomas, J. P.

Joshua Garner & Sallie Boon, m 24 Aug 1866 by W. L. Thomas, J. P.

Jos Muse(?) & E. J. Buie, m 1 May 1866 by M. Johnson, minister.

Thos Sanders & Ann E. Tally, m 18 Apr 1866 by M. Johnson, minister.

M. Shepherd & Margaret Dorsett, m 8 Aug 1866 by R. H. Marshall, minister.

James Fowler & Carlin Thomas, m 26 March 1866 by S. R. Perry, J. P.

Jas H. McMath & M. M. Dorsett, m 29 July 1866 by R. H. Marsh, minister.

N. Brewer & Nancy J. Boyd, m 12 July 1866 by E. H. McManis, J. P.

CHATHAM COUNTY NC MARRIAGES 1772-1868

Gilbert Poe & Mary A. Stone, m 28 March 1866 by Jas F. Rives, J. P.

Isaac H. Clegg & Sarah J. Bynum, m 15 Apr 1865 by William F. Clegg, minister.

Aaron Atwater & Bettie Norwood, m 26 Aug 1866 by H. H. Gibbons, minister.

David N. Teague & L. A. Hinshaw, m 23 Dec 1866 by H. G. Albright, J. P.

William Taylor & Jennie Alson, m 25 July 1868 by Daniel Black.

J. A. Cheek & Susan N. Merritt, m 18 Apr 1867 by J. P. Mason, minister.

Sidney Merritt & Helin Mason, m 10 Apr 1867 by W. C. Wilson, J. P.

John Buckanan & Jane Buckanan, m 7 Aug 1867 by A. Pattishall.

Eligey Merritt & Jane Trice, m 7 Aug 1867 by W. C. Wilson.

O. A. Hanner & Josephine Rives, m 13 Nov 1867 by A. J. Emerson.

G. A. Bryant & Nancy J. Riggsbee, m 9 Apr 1868 by J. D. Brasington, J. P.

Edmon Cotton (col) & Margaret Barnes, 5 Nov 1867 by M. C. Thomas, J. P.

Abner Brown & Susan Bennett, m 5 Sept 1867 by A. J. Riggsbee, J. P.

Cad Merritt & Dina Dollar, m 12 Oct 1867 by J. D. Brasington.

Edwin Horton & Margaret Hatch, m 6 Oct 1867 by J. D. Brasington.

James M. Williams & Phoebe C. Kirby, m 6 Aug 1868 by J. D. Brasington, J. P.

J. W. Caveness & Nancy A. Brady, m 23 Aug 1866 by J. S. Scott, J. P.

J. W. Breedlove & Harriet Wicker, m 23 March 186 by J. M. Stout, J. P.

CHATHAM COUNTY NC MARRIAGES 1772-1868

T. J. Griffin & Bettie Bland, m 8 Jan 1867 by G. P. Moore, J. P.

David Hammett & Elizar Hearn, m 2 Jan 1867 by G. P. Moore, J. P.

Richard Riddle & Jane Hancock, m 3 May 1867 by G. P. Moore, J. P.

Asa Thomas & Ann Boon, m 29 March 1868 by W. C. Thomas, J. P.

L. M. Brewer & Mary Paschal, m 1 May 1867 by R. H. Marsh, J. P.

J. A. Peoples & Fanny Frasier, m 23 Apr 1868 by Robt Sutton, minister.

William Ragland & Elizabeth Lawrence, m 4 March 1868 by Isaac W. Avent, minister.

Thos L. March & Mary Craton, m 6 Apr 1866 by William Griffin, J. P.

Moore (col) & Rachel Thompson (col), 15 Jan 1867 by __ Mallory, J. P.

H. T. Riggsbee & J. S. Burnet, m 14 Feb 1867 by C. C. Atwater, J. P.

Samuel Alston (col) & Early Perry, m 8 May 1868 by Wm Lineberry, minister.

Josiah Clark & Emily Lambert, m 8 Sept 1867 by J. M. Edwards, J. P.

Ambrose Eubanks & Antoinett Norwood, m 28 Apr 1868 by Thos B. Farrar.

Norman Rives (col) & Bettie Holmes (col), m 6 Feb 1868 by H. O. Dunlap.

Samuel Hendrix & Elizabeth Martin, m 10 May 1868 by H. O. Dunlap, J. P.

Solomon Lamb & Nancy Love, m 19 May 1867 by Samuel Bolan, minister.

Abner B. Roberson & Cornelia A. Stone, m 9 June 1867 by Saml Bolan, minister.

Jasper Mitchell & Fanny Stone, m 6 Jan 1867 by G. P. Moore, J. P.

Benjamin Brasington & Melly Green Riggsbee, m 12 Dec 1866 by G. P. Moore.

John A. Smith & Emeline Jones, m 18 May 1868 by A. J. Emerson.

Nat Loyd & Camelia Williams, m 17 Aug 1867 by A. B. Bright, J. P.

J. A. Crawford & Emeline Ferguson, m 21 Oct 1867 by Alson Gray.

M. L. Hackney & K. E. Peoples, m 23 Apr 1868 by A. J. Emerson.

Joseph Bond & Samantha Stewart, m 31 March 1867 by C. Goodwin, J. P.

H. C. Long & M. H. Crump, m 31 Nov 1867 by Robt Sutton, minister.

Henry Prince & E. H. Drake, m 27 Feb 1868 by W. P. Taylor.

Thos Carter & Mary J. Willet, m 24 Nov 1867 by R. R. Moore.

Albert Partin & Susan Mitchel, m 20 Oct 1867 by O. E. Harris, J. P.

John Campbell & Artelia Copeland, m 9 Feb 1868 by Josiah Stone.

F. A. Ramsay & A. S. Thompson, m 23 July 1868 by W. H. Bobbitt.

Joseph J. Fox & Elizabeth E. Dorsett, m 30 Apr 1867 by Wm. Lineberry, minister.

James Smith & Elizabeth Allen, m 25 Aug 1867 by H. O. Durham.

Robert Edwards & Elizabeth A. Bray, m 3 Jan 1868 by R. R. Moore.

J. M. Brooks & R. C. Edwards, m 1 Apr 1866 by R. R. Moore.

John Walden & Rattia Buckner, m 19 May 1867 by R. R. Moore.

Thomas Gardner & Louisa Holt, m 30 Apr 1868 by O. E. Harris, J. P.

Joseph Jones & Mary Crutchfield, m 14 apr 1868 by O. E. Harris, J. P.

CHATHAM COUNTY NC MARRIAGES 1772-1868

Ira Branton & Nancy McBane, m 14 Nov 1867 by Josiah Stone, J. P.

Bristoe Haughton & Fanny Perry, m 23 Sept 1866 by Wm Lineberry, minister.

Wm L. Hackney & Martha E. Dorsett, m 16 Aug 1866 by Wm Lineberry, minister.

M. B. Gilmore & Levina Thomas, m 26 July 1868 by Minter Johnson, minister.

Thos Pattishall (col) & Sue Jones (col), m 25 Dec 1866 by Minter Johnson.

Joseph Hicks & Margaret Bishop, m 3 Nov 1867 by J. M. Edwards.

John Wilkey & Jane Kelly, m 21 Dec 1867 by John A. Pattishall, J. P.

Archibald Wicker & Cornelia ODaniel, m 21 Aug 1867 by J. A. Pattishall, J. P.

John F. Ansley & Jerusha A. McIntyre, m 22 Dec 1867 by Minter Johnson.

Thomas Dunn & Margaret McJaggrett, m 8 July 1862 by Minter Johnson.

James Salmon & Sarah Willet, m 14 Nov 1867 by E. H. McMorris, J. P.

Ephraim Nixon & Lucy Goins, m 22 Oct 1867 by L. R. Perry, J. P.

Lee Battle & Elizabeth Harriss, m 20 Nov 1867 by W. H. Bobbitt.

A. D. Mason & Lizzie Sears, m 20 Dec 1866 by J. R> Mason, minister.

S. M. Beckwith & Mary Thrailkill, m 29 Nov 1866 by Willis C. Wilson, J. P.

W. H. Merritt & Anney Goodwin, m 31 Jan 1867 by Willis C. Wilson.

Y. A. Holt & Thena Poe, m 21 Feb 1867 by B. H. Woodell, J. P.

Aley Gilmore & Mary Bridges, m 6 Aug 1867 by Minter Johnson.

William Ivy & Ceny Bishop, m 2 Aug 1868 by T. Bolin.

Madison L. Clark & Frances Dowdy, m 24 Feb 1867 by Minter Johnson.

Dennis Dowdy & Polly A. Hart, m 11 Oct 1866 by Minter Johnson.

Thomas H. Burges & Hester A. Mitchel, m ___ 1867 by G. P. Moore, J. P.

James E. Watson & Annie Cariber, m 21 Jan 1868 by Minter Johnson.

J. M. Dickens & Aphia Loyd, m 8 Jan 1867 by Minter Johnson.

Mathias Dorsett & Mary E. Brewer, m 24 Dec 1867 by R. R. Moore.

A. M. Webster & Martha Lambert, m 27 Oct 1867 by R. R. Moore.

M. H. Wren & S. M. Johnson, m 31 June 1867 by P. M. Pickett, J. P.

George M. Brooks & Annie M. Clegg, m 19 Dec 1867 by W. H. Bobbitt.

Harrington Pope & Della A. Williams, m 22 Feb 1865 by Robt B. Sutton, M. G.

Jas. Fogleman & Sarah Simmons, m 23 Sept 1866 by W. G. Albright, J. P.

Winship Goodwin & Francis Council, m 20 Sept 1866 by James B. Long, minister.

Jesse Nelson & Mahala Overman, m 4 Nov 1866 by W. G. Albright, J. P.

Alvis Webster & Finetty Phillips, m 6 Dec 1867 by J. A. Scott, J. P.

A. N. Lineberry & Susan Fox, m 8 Sept 1867 by R. H. Marsh, minister.

William Bland & Mary Bright, m 8 Apr 1866 by William Griffin, J. P.

J. W. Womble & Frances A. Clark, m 18 Jan 1867 by G. P. Moore, J. P.

James T. Rogers & Susan W. Marsh, m 27 March 1866 by R. H. Marsh, minister.

William Womble & E. J. Hearn, m 20 Dec 1866 by J. N. Farrell.

Sidney Sauls & Mary J. Hinsley, m 6 Jan 1867 by Elias Bryan, J. P.

John O. Conner & Martha Johnson, m 20 Dec 1866 by E. Bryan, J. P.

John D. Wicker & Delitha Thomas, m 25 Sept 1864 by M. Johnson.

Joshua Glover & Jane Walace, m 28 Feb 1867 by Robt Marsh, minister.

J. D. Caudle & Louisa Adams, m 22 Jan 1867 by William G. Snipes, J. P.

J. H. Patterson & Alsy Jane Siler, m 26 March 1868 by Wm Lineberry, minister.

A. Cambell & Julia Clark, m 20 Nov 1866 by O. Clark, J. P.

John Unthank & Dinah Hinshaw, m 7 Oct 1866 by O. Clark, J. P.

Cesen Harris & Mahala Johnson, m 20 Jan 1867 by O. Clark, J. P.

W. J. Marsh & Matilda Hackney, m 10 Oct 1867 by Jas. A. Gilliland, J. P.

James Hatch & Rebecca Caudle, m 13 Jan 1867 by J. D. Brasington, J. P.

H. G. McBane & M. J. Stewart, m 22 Dec 1866 by O. Clark, J. P.

George Patterson & Sarah M. Turner, m 24 Jan 1867 by O. Clark, J. P.

C. R. Lambert & M. J. Claridy, m 9 Dec 1866 by R. R. Moore.

Benj Welsh & Lydia Jane Phillips, m 4 Nov 1866 by J. A. Scott, J. P.

John Judd & Francis Avent, m 6 Dec 1866 by Isaac W. Avent, pastor.

John Parish & Polly Ronsley, m 5 Sept 1866 by J. M. Stout, J. P.

James H. Kelly & Catharine Brown, m 13 Dec 1866 by Gaston Farrar, minister.

John Tenny & Martha Ward, m 24 Dec 1863 by J. M. Stout, J. P.

Logan Poe & Candis Smith, m 10 Jan 1866 by N. Farrell.

J. H. Thomas & Elizabeth Brown, m 8 Nov 1866 by H. W. Peoples, J. P.

John Evans & Elizabeth Brewer, m 14 Oct 1866 by James F. Rives, J. P.

David Stephens & Mary A. Stuart, m 24 Dec 1865 by H. O. Durham, J. P.

James H. Headen & M. E. Ramsey, m 22 Jan 1867 by W. H. Bobbitt.

Wm. J. Dowd & Mary M. Straughn, m 23 Dec 1867 by Wm Lineberry, minister.

Ephraim Emerson & Milley Rives (col), m 2 Jan 1868 by J. M. Bridges, J. P.

Joseph Emerson & Fanny Golston (col), m 22 Feb 1868 by J. M. Bridges, J. P.

George M. McCuller & Mary Malone, m 10 Aug 1864 by A. McIntyre, J. P. (license dated 8 Aug 1864)

James Dowdy & Mary A. Dowdy, m 7 March 1865 by A. McIntyre, J. P. (license dated 6 March 1865)

Brown Burke & Martha Barber, m 3 Aug 168 by A. McIntyre, J. P.

James Moore & Mary White, m 261 March 1861 by S. Gilmore.

Marshal Oldham & Francis Burke, m 3 June 1868 by A. McIntyre, J. P.

Baxter Gilmore & Sarah B. Beal, m 16 Jan 1860 by S. Gilmore.

Harris Hart & Elizabeth Oldham, m 16 Apr 1865 by A. McIntyre, J. P.

Samuel Moil & Merinda Gilmore, m 24 Apr 1861 by S. Gilmore.

A. B. Burns & Rachel Roser, m 6 Jan 1866 by Stephen Gilmore.

Calvin Holder & Eliza Munholand, m 15 Dec 1861 by E. P. Fearington, Esq.

Wm Jinkins (colored) & Eave Fearington, m 8 Aug 1867 by E. P. Fearington, J. P.

Wm H. Crabtree & Sarah A. Harwood, m 28 March 1867 by E. P. Fearington, J. P.

Jorden Fearington & Margaret Council, m 20 Feb 1868 by E. P. Fearington.

Charles Jourden & Nancy Buie, m 27 Dec 1865 by S. Gilmore.

John H. May & M. C. Burns, m 3 Dec 1865 by Stephen Gilmore.

James Mashburn & Nancy Tally, m 22 Feb 1863 by Z. A. Boroughs, J. P.

Hiram Wells & Catharine Thompson, m 25 March _____ by H. O. Durham.

Jacob Cook & Mary Johnson, m 28 Nov 1867 by W. R. McMath, J. P.

John M. Ellis & Rebecca J. Welch, m 9 Oct 1862 by Z. A. Boroughs, J. P.

Alvis Foust & Nancy Isley, m 24 Feb 1866 by H. O. Durham, J. P.

Jerry Lane (col) & Tabitha Lane (col), m 1 Dec 1867 by Jas. A. Gilleland, J. P.

Sampson Buntin & Elizabeth Johnson, m 1 Dec 1869 by W. R. McMath, J. P.

Edward Thompson & Matilda Whitehead, m 25 March 1866 by J. M. Stout, J. P.

John Moore & Lucinda E. Stout, m 13 May 1866 by H. O. Durham, J. P.

Isaiah Cole & Eliza A. Blake, m 19 March 1866 by J. B. Farrar, J. P.

Lewis Whitehead & Hariet Bell, m 16 Oct 1866.

John A. Williams & Margaret E. Stedman, m 6 Aug 1865 by J. A. McDonald, J. P.

Winship Clark & Elizabeth Goodwin, m 22 March 1866 by James B. Long.

Phillip Faucett & Mary Ansley, m 4 Dec 1865 by B. H. Jones, J. P.

S. H. Carter & Sarah Dixon, m 20 Oct 1867 by H. O. Durham, J. P.

Lucian Neal & Kissiah Caudle, m 10 May 1866.

J. G. Small & Clara Cowan, m 18 Feb 1866.

R. C. Siler & Susan E. Mathews, m 3 May 1866 by Wm Lineberry, minister.

Daniel S. Watkins & Naby Thomlinson, m 25 July 1865 by J. A. McDonald, J. P.

N. B. Gunter & H. W. Stedman, m 6 Aug 1865 by G. P. Moore, J. P.

Joseph D. Hackney & Sarah J. Dorsett, m 23 Jan 1866 by Wm Lineberry, minister.

William Clemens & E. A. Williams, m 2 Jan 1868 by W. C. Wilson, J. P.

Thos Ward & Nancy J. Hill, m 12 Dec 1861 by Z. A. Boroughs, J. P.

John Garrey & Mary Marshburn, m 8 June 1863 by Z. A. Boroughs, J. P.

Wm. Hackney & Emma Poe, m 19 July 1865 by G. P. Moore, J. P.

Joseph Brady & Mary Hix, m 17 Jan 1861 by Z. A. Boroughs, J. P.

CHATHAM COUNTY NC MARRIAGES 1772-1868

Green Tally & M. Bridges, m 12 March 1861 by Z. A. Boroughs, J. P.

Aaron Hilliard & Lydia McManus, m 1 Feb 1862 by Z. A. Boroughs, J. P.

Joseph Emerson & Fanny Goldston, m 22 Feb 1868 by J. M. Bridges, J. P.

Ephram Emerson & Mollie Rives, m 2 June 1868 by J. M. Bridges, J. P.

Nathan Brafford & Hannah Perry, m 15 Oct 1866.

Jesse Palmer & Sarah Palmer, m 14 July 1866.

D. W. Morris & Candice T. Smith, m 19 Oct 1866 by W. M. Tally, J. P.

Wm. H. McDonald & Lydia Smith, m 10 Jan 1867 by W. M. Tally, J. P.

G. T. Hart & Ann Wilkie, m 17 Sept 1867 by W. M. Tally, J. P.

Andrew Crain & Nancy Temples, m 5 Sept 1867 by William Griffin, J. P.

John L. Hinton & Iona Horton, m 1 Aug 1867 by William Griffin, J. P.

Stephen R. Burnett (col) & Annie Fearington, m 27 Aug 1867.

Alfonso Richardson & Annie Thrailkill, m in New Hope Township, Chatham Co, NC, m 21 Nov 1867 by Rev. James B. Long, Methodist minister. (recorded May 20 1914)

Bird (cont.)
  James Washington 69
  Nancy 5
Bishop, Ceny 102
  Margaret 101
  Tabitha 74
Black, Daniel 98
  Murdoc 82
Blackston, Mary 25
Blake, Eliza A. 106
Blalock, Fanny 6
  Julius 79
Bland, Bettie 99
  Eugenia 87
  Grady 9
  Hiram 94
  John 63
  Mary 13
  Mary W. 92
  Matilda D. 61
  Rebecca 57
  Thomas 2
  William 102
Bobbit, W. H. 90
  W. H. (Rev.) 86, 89
Bobbitt, W. H. 100, 101,
  102, 104
Bocame, Eliza 39
Boggs, Jos 95
  Mary 51
  Solomon 66
Bolan, Saml (Rev.) 99
  Samuel (Rev.) 99
Bolding, Mary A. 82
Bolin, T. 102
Boling, Cynthia 57
  Dilla 12
  Elizabeth 41
  Nicholas 41
  T. (Rev.) 45, 50
Bond, Joseph 100
Booker, Patsey 25
Boon, Ann 99
  Betsey 14
  C. A. (Rev.) 91, 92
  Elizth 55
  Henry 64
  J. W. 46
  Jehu 44
  Matilda 26, 63
  Nathan 50
  Sallie 97
  Wiley J. 63
Boroughs, James 95
  Z. A. 70, 75, 76, 78,
    79, 105, 106, 107
Borrow, Sarah E. 38
Borwn, F. M. 81
Bouroughs, John 85
Bowden, Geo. W. 78
  Peggy 85
  William 67
Bowen, Julia Ann 43
Bowlin, A. T. 19
Boyd, Murphy 40
  Nancy J. 97
  William 2
Boylan, Samuel M. 6
Bradors, Nancy 27
Brady, Joseph 106
  Nancy 24
  Nancy A. 98
  Nelson 11
  Thos 90
Braffon, Stephen 47
Brafford, Mary 56
  Nathan 107
Brandly, Brooks 7

Brannon, Abner 80
Branson, Henry 65
  Polly 96
Brantley, Mary 4
  Susan 55
  William 4
Brantly, Brooks 20
  Elizabeth 8
  Mary 4
  Susan 59
  William 4
Branton, Ira 101
Brasington, Benjamin 100
  Francis 83
  J. C. D. 73
  J. D. 53, 85, 86, 87,
    89, 91, 98, 103
  J. R. 87
  Jane 26, 39
  Joseph D. 74, 79
  Joseph P. 83
  M. C. 47
  Samuel 24
Braxton, Elisha 21
  Jonathan 61
Bray, Angelet 50
  Ann 3
  Ann E. 47
  Calvin D. 8
  Edward 23
  Elizabeth 23
  Elizabeth A. 100
  Fanny 23
  Henry 3
  James 3
  Jaob H. 60
  Jer. D. 3
  Joab 70
  Joab H. 59, 70
  John (Jr.) 3
  Julia A. 80
  Mark 4
  Mary 9, 23
  Mary E. 95
  Nancy 25
  Nathan B. 43
  Patsy 4
  Ruth N. 53
  Susan 11
  William 3
Breedlove, J. W. 98
Brewer, Allen 2
  Amey 75
  Elizabeth 26, 104
  Green 63
  Jeremiah 3
  John 4, 6, 18, 36
  L. M. 99
  Lydia 54
  Martha 70
  Mary 90
  Mary E. 60, 102
  N. 97
  Oliver 19
  Rebecca 18
  S. G. 52
  Samuel 85
  Wm 50
  Wm. G. 92
Brewster, M. J. 88
Bridges, Adeline 70
  Bethena P. 80
  H. D. 1
  Horace D. 3
  J. M. 104, 107
  M. 107
  Mary 102
  Nicholas 33

Bright, A. B. 100
  Alvis 69
  Caly 3
  Gemima 35
  Isaac 86
  John R. 65
  Lenora J. 71
  Lucy 20, 73
  Mary 2, 102
  Nancy 19
  Oliver 14
  Sina J. 94
Briles, W. 50
Britt, Julia E. M. (?)
  69
Britton, Emily 85
Brock, Joseph J. 34
Brooks, Callie E. 96
  Eliza J. 13
  Emily J. 3
  Fanny 18
  Flora A. 61
  George M. 102
  Isaac T. 65
  J. M. 100
  J. T. 96
  James 11, 33
  John M. 47
  Larkin 29
  Lydia B. 33
  Mary 7
  Nancy 29
  Parker 7
  Rebecca 18
  Richard 14
  Ruth 7, 14
  Sallie E. 96
  Sally 5
  Sally H. 3
  Sarah 3
  Susan 47
  Susanna 14
  Thos A. 72, 87
  Timothy T. 3, 18
  William T. 36
  Wm. H. 95
Broughs, Z. A. 65
Brown, Abner 98
  Alfred 63
  Allston 17
  Alvis 84
  Annah J. 84
  Burwell W. 83
  Catharine 104
  Daniel 27
  David C. 77
  Elijah 50
  Elizabeth 38, 104
  F. M. 81
  G. E. 51, 67, 71, 77
  G. E. (Rev.) 43, 45,
    49, 53, 62, 80
  James 1
  John 39
  Leah 36
  Luther 53
  Mary 40, 48
  Mary A. 49
  Mary E. 73
  Milly 31
  Phoebe 67
  Reeny 36
  Solomon 57
  Thomas M. 79
  William H. 75
Browning, Martin 53
  William 63
Browyers, Paulina 49

Brwon, G. E. 71
Bryan, Benjamine R. 80
  E. 89, 96, 103
  Elias 49, 63, 76, 90,
    96, 103
Bryant, Elias 38, 59, 68
  G. A. 98
  Julia 64
  Mary M. 86
  William 2, 43
  Wm 85
Buchanan, Sally 12
Buchannon, Flora Jane 44
  Griza J. 38
  Martha 4
Buchanon, Grissy Ann 34
  Semanthy 21
  Witty 34
Buchhannon, Louisa M. 66
Buchner, Jane (?) 35
Buck, H. H. 85
Buckanan, Jane 98
  John 98
Buckhanan, Hilliard S.
  67
  Nancy 85
Buckhannan, Fanny 16
Buckhannon, R. 65
Buckner, Edward 45
  Henry 50
  Jesse J. 80
  John 28
  Manly 80
  Mary Ann 38
  Nancy 84
  Rattia 100
  Thomas 81
Buie, E. J. 97
  Nancy 105
Bullard, Alsa 7
  Emily 95
  Hesperan 64
Buma, John 89
Bunn, Lydia 28
Buntin, Sampson 105
Bunting, Rebecca 25
Buntyne, Ebenezer 17
Burges, A. R. 65
  James 72
  Salinah 77
  Thomas H. 102
  Wm. A. 83
Burgess, A. R. 65
  Wm. R. 49
Burk, Eliza Ann 90
  H. H. 97
  Lovey 96
Burke, Brown 104
  Elizabeth 49
  Francis 104
  H. 70
  H. H. 4, 29, 80
  J. C. 78, 86
  Jeana 67
  Julia 87
  Martha 71
  Mary 49
  Miller 50
  Nancy 29
  Rachel M. 75
  Robert 41
  Timothy B. 81
  Willliam 17
Burne, Permelia F. 90
Burnet, J. S. 99
  L. (Rev.) 57
Burnett, Atlas A. 31
  John 95

Burnett (cont.)
  John F. (Rev.) 96
  L. 68, 90
  L. (Rev.) 29, 38, 42,
    53, 66, 81, 82, 83,
    91
  Lucian 31
  Lucian (Rev.) 63
  Stephen R. 107
Burnette, L. (Rev.) 53
Burnitt, Julia 1
Burns, A. B. 105
  A. C. 64
  A. J. 56
  Amanda 46
  Ann E. 64
  Cornelia 95
  Eliza C. 57
  Elizabeth 40, 63
  Emaline 22
  Hannah B. 74
  Happy 35
  Henrietta 4
  Henry 32
  Henry C. 12
  Lavinia 4
  M. C. 105
  Margaret 28, 40
  Mary 13, 32
  May L. 78
  Micajah 22
  Reddek 30
  Robert 95
  Robt M. 97
  W. M. 38
  William M. 64
  Winney A. 26
  Winny Ann 45
Buroghs, A. 63
Buroughs, Z. A. 105
Burrows, M. A. 54
Buthrie, Beverly 30
Byans, Elizabeth 61
Bynum, Caroline 70
  Elizabeth 81
  J. H. 54
  Joseph 5
  Julia F. 86
  Lee 56
  Luke 38
  M. 62, 74, 83
  Margarett A. 82
  Sarah J. 98
  Sarah N. 76
  Susan 5
  T. 60, 61, 75
  Turner 5
Byrd, Dolly 47
Cagle, Riley 79
Calburn, S. T. 51
Caldwell, C. K. (Rev.)
  90
  O. K. (Rev.) 82
Cambell, A. 103
Camel, Affiah 90
  Frances 71
  Thomas 81
Cammel, A. F. 81
Campbell, A. A. 92
  Caroline 92
  Delilah 29
  Elizabeth 69
  James P. 87
  Jane 33
  Jessee 96
  John 100
  John M. 90
  Mary A. 81

Campbell (cont.)
  Thomas 72
  W. C. 5
  William C. 33
Canter, Franky 32
  Jones 32
Cariber, Annie 102
Carlile, Robert 30
Carlisle, Rebecca 12
  Wm. 20
Carmicle, Martha An 82
Carny, J. 77
Carpenter, Robert 77
Carroll, E. W. 36
  Lydia B. 36
Carter, Ann 33
  B. W. 9
  Gilliam 42, 85
  Gillim 97
  Hannah J. 38
  John (Jr.) 28
  Jonathan 26
  Letha R. 72
  Louisa J. 13
  Love 36
  S. H. 106
  Salley 26
  Samuell 38
  Sarah 6
  Simri 30
  Thomas G. 7, 8, 33
  Thos 100
  W. A. 65
  W. B. 46, 49, 50, 55,
    56, 58, 60, 62, 65,
    74, 92, 94
  William 67
Cass, Polly 74
Castleberry, Micajah 73
Cate, Richard 7
Cater, W. B. 50
Caucy, Alexander 90
Caudle, David 48
  J. D. 103
  Kissiah 106
  Rebecca 103
  Wm. 91
Causey, Joshua 55, 65
Causy, John E. (?) 60
Caveness, J. W. 98
Caveny, Rebecca 50
Caviness, Anna 33
  Ransom 33
Chadwick, J. W. 63
Chaffin, W. S. (Rev.)
  65, 66
Chamness, Frances 29
Chapman, Charity 22
  Deberry 7, 22
  Lydia 2
Chavas, Nancy 5
Chavis, Pete 5
Cheak, Cathrine 79
  Elizabeth 71
  Hannah 78
  Joshua T. 71
  Mary 59
  T. W. 70
Cheek, Cleopatra 86
  J. A. 98
  John 27
  Nancy 85, 86
  Robert 86
Cheuss, Elizabeth (?) 36
Chick, Brooks 51
Church, H. O. 91
  O. (Rev.) 91
Churchil, O. (Rev.) 81

Churchill, Mary 77
  O. 54, 72, 76, 78, 80
  O. (Rev.) 82
Claiborn, Henry 4
Claridy, M. J. 103
Clark, Delia L. 61
  Delilah 26
  Eliza A. 51
  Elizabeth 7, 9, 48
  Enoch 64
  Frances A. 103
  Green 87
  J. 51, 52
  Jane 53
  Jemima 42
  John 48
  Johnathan 50
  Jonathan 5
  Joshua 77
  Josiah 99
  Julia 103
  Maben G. 78
  Madison L. 102
  Martha 44
  Mary 31
  Milly 5
  Nancy 14
  Nathan 74
  O. 51, 66, 69, 72, 85,
    86, 90, 95, 96, 97,
    103
  Oliver 67, 69, 72, 86
  Patsey 5
  Salina 57
  Susan 4
  Thomas B. 26
  Thos 14
  William 2, 29, 31
  Winship 106
Clarke, Hasseltine 57
  Johnson 84
  O. 56, 62, 82, 94
  Thomas 94
Cledenan, Mary Ann 48
Clegg, Ann 87
  Annie M. 102
  C. B. 66
  Isaac H. 98
  J. N. 76
  Luther 3, 61
  Margaret 5
  Margaret J. 64
  Mary 5
  S. 89
  Thomas J. 71
  William F. (Rev.) 98
Clemens, William 106
Climy, Sunnett 78
Cloud, Jonathan 18
Coble, Cathrine 65
  David 24
  Henry M. 97
  Herman 88
  Mebane 49
  Tempy 35, 42
Codle, Elizabeth 15
Coggin, Hollen 8
  James 78
  John 8
Coggins, D. W. 78
  Sally 52
Cole, (?) 11
  Bella 95
  Isaiah 106
  James 47
  John 37
  Jos. B. 60
  Nancy 7

Cole (cont.)
  W. B. 77
Coltrane, Owen 77
Colur, Polly 31
Conaby, Elizabeth 74
Conner, John O. 103
Conselman, Polly 1
Cook, Hannah 23
  Jacob 105
  Samantha 78
Cooper, Camma 80
  Elizabeth 80
  James 45
  Mary 69
  Matthew 6
  Oliver H. 90
  William 37, 59
Coose, Mary 39
Copeland, Artelia 100
  Bethana 74
  Esperann 43
  Gadis 63
  George 56
  Gideon 66
  Levi 66
  Malinda 78
Copland, Emeline 68
Copper, Mary C. 71
Coshall, Darios 20
Coshatt, Dorcas 18
Cotten, H. J. 55, 57
  Henry J. 59
  Mary 12
  R. C. 19
  Rhoderick 19
  Richard C. 30
  W. 51
Cotton, Ady (?) 91
  Angeline 77
  Edmon 98
  J. C. 39
  R. C. 15, 86
  Sally 12
Cottrell, Thomas 29
Council, A. C. 65
  Calvin L. 70
  Caroline U. 72
  Francis 102
  H. 56, 93
  Harriet 93
  Margaret 105
  R. C. 54, 70, 72, 75,
    77, 82, 83, 84
  Rebecca A. 70
  Thomas C. 83
  Walter C. 72
Covet, Horater 44
  Nicholas 56
Cowan, Clara 106
Cowen, Mag M. 84
Cox, Hannah 35
  Henry 45
  Jane 28
  John 17, 49
  Joseph 91
  Thomas C. 76
  Wm. 18
  Zacharias 20
Crabtree, Wm H. 105
Crain, Andrew 107
Crane, Kitty 36, 45
Craton, Elizabeth 85
  Mary 99
  Polly 28
Craven, Eliza 5
  Martha 70
Crawford, J. A. 100
Crayton, Robt 38

Crewes, L. B. 48
Croaker, William F. 42
Croker, John 43
Crosby, James N. 32
Cross, Francis 56
  Polly 5
  Sarah H. 83
Crow, James 40
Cruchfield, Mary A. 82
  W. C. 92
Crump, M. H. 100
  William 7
Crumpton, Oranna B. 67
Crutchfield, Benjamin 48
  Diamah 7
  Elizabeth 23, 35, 50
  Elizth 55
  Henry 7
  Jane A. 57
  Jesse 21
  Lilian 51
  Mahaly 29
  Martha 53
  Mary 29, 100
  Nancy 37
  R. J. 51
  Rebecca 17
  S. A. 97
  Sallie 89
  Sally 8
  Samuel H. 26
  Sarah E. 73
  Solomon D. 32
Cudle, James 36
Culberson, Ann 70
  Avelissa 54
  Jane 65
  John 33
  Margarett 93
  Phoebe A. 54
  S. T. 57, 58
  Sally 18
  Samuel 7
  Susannah 8
  T. S. 56
  William 18
Culbertson, Mariah 22
  Samuel T. 42
Culbreath, S. T. 50, 51
Cummings, Martha 23
Curl, Audner (?) 40
  Hannah 5
Dabney, John 4
Dafford, John H. 92
Daniel, Jesse 8
  Joseph 84
  Louisa M. 54
Dark, J. H. 79
  Mary 74
  Milly 20
  Nancy 18
  Nancy A. 21
  Polly 21
  Thomas 28
  Willis 21
  Winnafred 7
Darke, William H. 81
Daughordy, Sally 32
Davidson, Hannah 17
  John 34
  Rachel 30
Davis, Abba 77
  Cannon 15
  Easther 79
  F. S. 88
  Jane 15, 43
  Josiah 86
  Madison 88

Davis (cont.)
  May 22
  Nancy 59
  Sarah 48
  William 17
Dawson, Allas 40
  Joseph 40
  William 58
De Graffinreidt, Pamelia
  1
De Wright, Kate 94
Dean, Elisha 50
  John 28
Deaton, Mary 65
  Minty 18
  Selanee 80
  Winny 63
Denison, C. B. 84
Derham, Seban 57
Desern, Lewis 84
Dickens, Frances 64
  J. M. 102
  John D. 80
  Mac 58
  Polly 30
Dickson, Elizabeth 48
  John 55
Discer, Joshua 45
Dismukes, Alexander H.
  23
  Amelia A. 53
  Celia 96
  Elisha 53
  Elizabeth 63, 66
  Joseph 57
  Raechel 13
Dixon, Catharine 84
  David 12
  Joseph 87
  Mary 85
  Nathan 85
  Rachel 44
  Sarah 106
  Thos C. 53
Dodd, Alexander 8, 30
  Fanny 93
  George 14
  Hannah 30
Dollar, Dina 98
  Jonathan 27
Doller, Tapley 8
Done, George 70
Dorest, Hezekiah 35
Dorset, Duty 8
  Eliza 34
  Francis 28
  Hezekiah 18
  John 5
  Maria 30
Dorsett, E. R. 97
  Elizabeth 11
  Elizabeth Ann 81
  Elizabeth E. 100
  Henry 24
  Joseph 13
  M. M. 97
  Margaret 97
  Martha E. 101
  Mathias 102
  Milly 13
  Polly 44
  R. 83, 85, 87
  Rosanna 45
  Sarah J. 106
  Susanna 13
Dosett, O. M. 91
  Susan 68
Doud, Affiat 75

Douglas, Elizabeth 83
  Silas J. 83
Dove, Nancy 79
Dowd, A. S. 41, 43, 50,
  51, 55
  Atlas 35
  Emeline G. 50
  F. W. 19
  Francis 24
  G. W. 42
  James C. 76
  Leah P. 25
  Lydia 36
  Mariah 11
  Owen 17
  P. W. (Rev.) 41
  Rosanah 82
  T. C. 50
  Wm. J. 104
Dowde, Charles 90
Dowdy, Barsheba 5
  Dennis 102
  Frances 102
  Hezekiah 75
  James 8, 104
  John 6
  Mary A. 104
  Mathew 83
  Phebe 44
  S. H. 89
  Sally 32
  Thomas W. 61
  Thos 55
  William 27
  Wm. 16
  Wm. T. 83
Drake, E. H. 100
  Elizabeth 72
  Gabriel 71
  George 20
  Hesperan 69
  John B. 10
  Louisa A. 39
  Sally 52
  Silva I. 13
  Vetra 90
  Virginia 53
Draton, John 49
Drumond, Benjamin 16
Duke, Henry M. 58
Duman, William A. 80
Duncan, David 46
  Martha K. 68
  Micajah 31
  William 89
Dungil, John 8
Dunken, Polly 32
Dunlap, H. O. 54, 93, 99
  N. B. 48, 55, 69
Dunn, Thomas 101
Durham, Alexander 42
  H. A. 75
  H. O. 78, 84, 85, 87,
    88, 93, 95, 96, 100,
    104, 105, 106
  Jane 62
  M. O. 83
  Martha 42
  Mary Ann 85
  Rena 27
Eason, Sarah Jane 34
Edards, Polly 17
Edmunds, Samson 49
Edwards, A. 51
  Betsey 10
  Catharine 43
  Cornelius 73
  Eliza 29

Edwards (cont.)
  Emeline 46
  Hannah 2
  Henry 69
  Irvin 43
  Issabell 3
  J. M. 99, 101
  J. N. 9
  Jemimah 9
  Joshua 9
  Joshua (Jr.) 17
  Margy 15
  Maria 1
  Martha 18, 36, 43
  Martha T. 28
  Nathan 3
  Peggy 30
  Polly 17
  R. C. 100
  Rachel 8, 19
  Robert 14, 100
  S. 44, 50, 58
  Sally M. 68
  Samson 43, 71
  Samuel B. 9
  Stokes 9
  Stokes B. 50
  Thos A. 54
  W. S. 89, 93, 94
  W. Y. 96
  William S. 2, 11, 18
  Wm A. 63
  Wm. S. 68
Elitt, J. F. 76
Elke, Laura C. (?) 74
Elkins, Bettie 86
  Elizabeth 79
  John 69
  Lewis 12
  Mary 54
  Rebecca 51
  Samuel 28
  Sarah 75
Ellett, Sarah A. 85
Ellington, George B. 45
  George W. 9
  M. E. 93
  Sally 2
  Sarah J. 88
  W. E. 81
Elliott, Micajah 8
Ellis, Alfred 93
  Hansel 48
  John M. 105
  Lemuel 88, 93
  Mary 53
  Minerva 52
  Nancy 92
  Richard 54
  Sarah 82
  Wm H. 95
Ellmoor, Arther 96
Elmer, Joanna 50
Elmore, Cornelia 87
  Elizabeth 44
  Emily 52
  John 82
  Joseph 9
  M. G. 93
  Mary Ann 5
  Wm 55
Emberson, John M. 82
Emerson, A. J. 76, 95,
  98, 100
  A. J. (Rev.) 87, 93
  Aaron 50
  Betsey 5
  Ephraim 104

Hargrove, Elizabeth 56
  John 5
Harlle, Wm. F. 87
Harman, Efreann C. 38
  Elizabeth 50
  Elizabeth E. 84
  James H. 14
  Jane 57
  John 4, 13, 20
  M. F. 95
  Mary A. 63
  Sarah 17
  Sina 44
  William 77
Harper, Edward 14
  W. W. 72
Harrington, A. J. 73
  Sally 26
  Whitmill 28
Harris---, Elizabeth 12
Harris, Alvis 45
  Benjamin 92
  Cesen 103
  Cornelia 15, 87
  Edward 71
  Elisha 6
  Elizabeth 12, 83
  Emma 95
  Lydia M. 61
  Martha 14, 42
  Mary J. 46
  Nancy 4
  O. E. 100
  Oscar 42
  Ruth 13
  Sallie H. 81
  Sally 9
  W. G. 40, 45, 46, 48,
    62, 64, 67, 73, 80
  W. T. 64
  Wm. 79
  Wm. G. 46, 67
Harriss, Elizabeth 10,
  101
  W. G. 55
Hart, Affa J. 47
  Blakely 84
  Dilly 12
  Elisha 62
  G. T. 107
  Harris 105
  John 25
  Lucy 77
  Merrell 27
  Merrill 12
  Polly 12
  Polly A. 102
  Thomas 14
  Vinton 73
  Yeargin 56
Hartsal, Hannah 31
Hartsatte, Disa 30
Harward, Lewis M. 62
Harwood, Elizabeth 22
  J. H. 81
  Kiddy 61
  Martha 61
  Sarah A. 105
Hashal, Elizabeth 66
Hasken, Phillip W. 72
Hasler, William J. (?)
  79
Hat, Agnes F. 23
Hatch, Elizabeth 2
  Elizabeth B. 71
  Emeline 44
  Francis 87
  G. W. 69

Hatch (cont.)
  Henry 90
  J. H. 88
  J. W. 45, 47, 48, 50,
    53, 63, 64, 66, 69,
    74, 87, 88
  James 103
  John W. 63, 68, 81
  M. F. 95
  Margaret 98
  Mary Ann 53, 93
  Sydney 27
  Tabitha 91
  W. 43
  William 53
Hatcock, E. 95
Hathcock, James 52
Hatley, Loami 93
  R. 43
  Redding 15
  Salitha 93
  Tabitha 9
  Yoma 93
Hatly, R. 48
  Tacitia 88
Hatt, Alexander 18
Hatwood, Alfred 1
  Clara 39
  Edner 69
  Mary 1, 39
Haughton, Bristoe 101
  M. C. 90
  M. M. 57
Hawkins, John (Rev.) 89
  John H. 1, 20
Haywood, William 64
Headen, A. D. 47, 48,
  51, 52
  A. G. 48, 54, 60
  A. Gaston 15, 41, 46
  A. H. 68
  Aaron D. 13, 18
  Andrew 40
  Ann 54
  Atlas J. 83
  Celia 54
  James H. 104
  Josiah 4, 12
  Martha L. 40
  Mary Etta 93
  Minerva 45
  Sally 25
  Susannah 7
  William F. 79
Headin, A. B. 58
  John Q. 73
  Polly 1
  Sarah A. 72
Hearen, Louisa 17
Hearin, Tynerah 25
Hearitt, Edwin A. 25
Hearn, A. G. 95
  Alvan 79
  Basil 68
  E. J. 103
  Elizar 99
  Howel 43
  Louisa 17
  Margaret 59
  Mary T. 25
Heath, A Gaston (?) 44
Heathcock, Franklin 61
Heathcocok, Eliza 58
Heflin, R. F. (Rev.) 47
  R. T. 49
  R. T. (Rev.) 47, 48
Henderson, Camelia 42
  Caroline 95

Henderson (cont.)
  Caroline 47
  Elizabeth 51
  Isaac 44
  J. E. 79
  James 67, 90
  John 5
  Mary 58
  Nancy 72, 82
  Obediah B. 5
  Wiley 15
  Wm. 94
Hendricks, Reuben 11
Hendrix, Samuel 99
Henry, Mary 89
Henshaw, Hannah 15
  Margaret 5
Henson, Robert 11
Hensy, Thomas 65
Herndon, Betty 30
  John 25
  Mary Jane 60
Herring, Beda 15
Heube, A. Dallas 44
Hickman, Abigal 93
  Geo. 71
Hicks, Joseph 101
  Lasker B. 59
  Sophia 70
  Spencer 70
  Wesley 22, 23
  Wilby 12
Higdon, Susannah 4
Hill, John 35
  Luraner 7
  Mariah R. 77
  Nancy J. 106
  Polly 35
  Susan 69
  Thomas N. 79
  Wm. H. 83
Hillard, Nathan 86
Hilliard, Aaron 107
  Joseph 41
  Lovey 48
  W. M. 42
  William S. 70
Hinesley, Lucy A. 52
Hinkman, George 49
Hinley, William 85
Hinshaw, Abigail 32
  Barzalla 74
  Benjamin 15, 24
  Daniel 69
  Dinah 103
  Elizabeth 32
  Jesse 21, 27
  John 15
  John (Rev.) 67, 68,
    69, 74, 88, 94, 97
  Josiah 15
  L. A. 98
  Lidia 89
  Mary Jane 77
  Thomas 23
  Thos 56
Hinsley, Eliza 7
  Mary J. 103
Hinsly, James 41
Hinson, Nancy 48
  Thos V. 94
  Uriah 23
Hinton, A. G. 39
  John L. 62, 107
  Mary A. 57
Hix, Mary 106
Hobby, Alexander 75
  William J. 57

McMath (cont.)
  Mary 57
  O. 43, 44, 50, 55, 56,
    67, 82
  Oliver 70
  Robert R. 6, 10, 14,
    15
  Susan 44
  W. R. 105
McMorris, E. H. 101
  E. H. (?) 92
McNair, Evander 57
McNeill, Agness W. 30
McNiell, Leml S. 19
McPeter, A. 75
McPherson, Aaron 56
  Catharine 56
  Cornelius 14
  David 21
  Delilah 11
  Edah 67
  James 21
  Margaret 29
  Martha 49
  Mary 61
  Nancy 14
  Oliver 43
  Phebe 2
  Rebecca 17
  Ruthy 28
  Sarah 26
  William 21
McRae, C. C. 87
Mciver, D. F. 72, 73
Meacham, Elizabeth 56
Melton, N. 57
Merritt, Cad 98
  Eligey 98
  Pleasant 25
  Sidney 98
  Susan N. 98
  W. H. 101
Meyer, Sarah P. 60
Micher, John 96
Miller, Elizabeth 73
  Lidda 46
  Mary Ann 92
  William 31
Millican, Elias 22
Milton, N. 59, 63
Mimms, Anna 51
  B. 51
  B. S. 53
  S. 46
  Thos Q. 68
Mims, B. L. 72
  B. S. 58, 60, 69
  Barzilla 41
  Carney 74
  W. J. 89
Minten, Martha A. 22
Minter, Richard 22
  T. J. 61
Mirack, Mary 94
Mirich, Kiriss (?) 17
Mitchel, Calvin 70
  Celia A. 79
  Hester A. 102
  Sion 72
  Susan 100
  William A. 71
Mitchell, Catharine 17
  Elizabeth 85
  Jane 39
  Jasper 100
  Nancy 14, 44
  Thomas 52
  William 23

Mitchell (cont.)
  Wm. R. 96
Mitchum, Elizabeth 47
Mobly, Pyrana M. 94
Moffet, Dennis 47
Moffit, E. A. 95
  John 81
Moil, Samuel 105
Monroe, Jos 91
Montgomery, Deborah 7
  John 7, 33
Moody, (?) 66
  Gilly 23
  Henry 73
  Jones 33
  Josiah 24
  Kezziah S. 9
  Mariah 10
  Mary E. 55
  Nathl 53
  Rebecca 33
  Riley 23
  Timothy J. 69
  William 2, 25, 33, 35,
    36
  Wm. 9, 30
Moon, Andrew 16
  Andrew J. 62
  Ann 15
  Ann J. 7
  Caroline 9, 16
  Eliza A. 75
  Hannah 15
  James 2
  John 23
  Jonathan 23
  Joseph 23
  Margaret 38
  Mary W. 62
  Polly 36
  Simon 23
Moore, (?) 99
  Ann 63
  Elisha A. 44
  Emalne 95
  Esperan 73
  F. M. 96
  G. P. 93, 99, 100,
    102, 103, 106
  Henry T. 73
  James 104
  John 106
  John D. 48
  Joseph J. 62
  Mary 1
  R. R. 100, 102, 103
  R. R. (Rev.) 90
  Richard B. 84
  Richard K. (Rev.) 83
  Richard R. 72
  Richard R. (Rev.) 83
  Sarah 32
  Winny 17
  Wm. 46
  Wm. (Jr.) 85
  Wm. B. 52
Moran, Samuel M. 91
  Susan 89
  Wm 49
Morand, Chloe 2
  Polly 33
Morgan, D. 91
  Jones 31
  Martha 69
  Patte 63
  Sherod 67
  Zachariah H. 74
Morrer, Thomas R. 76

Morris, D. W. 107
  T. J. 92
  William H. 73
Morse, Elenor (?) 43
Moses, T. C. (Rev.) 88,
  91
Moss, Letisha 15
  Thomas C. (Rev.) 59
Muckle, Elizabeth 45
Mulholland, Henderson 45
Mulloy, Edward 8
Mung, Nancy (?) 46
Munholand, Eliza 105
Munholland, Barb 88
Murcheson, Alexander 6
Murchison, Alexander 8
  D. C. 89, 90
  Henrietta 92
Murkerson, D. C. 89
Murray, Danl 53
  Sarah 56
Murry, Nelly M. 48
  Spencer 67
Muse, Jos (?) 97
Myrack, Saphrona A. P.
  95
Myrick, Duncan 39
  Joseph 63
  William L. 75
Nall, Dorcas 27
  Irvin 69
  J. W. 55
  Winship 93
Nalls, M. E. 91
  Rebecca 33
Nash, W. A. 13
Nation, Cinthia Caroline
  69
Neal, Ann 53
  Atlas 95
  Dilly 16
  E. M. 64
  Eliza 65
  Elizabeth 27, 39
  Elizabeth J. 91
  Isaiah 9
  Jane 25
  John 2, 7
  Lucian 106
  M. J. 86
  Martha 64
  Nacy J. 52
  Polly 53
Neil, Stephen 24
Nelson, Alvice A. 38
  Alvis 68
  Hannah (Mrs.) 24
  Jesse 102
  Margaret 94
  Pheby 88
  Polly 10
Nevells, Alfred 63
Newland, Sarah 22
Nicholson, Larkin 24
Night, Neal 30
Nigion, Josiah 62
Nixon, Ephraim 101
Norwood, Antoinett 99
  Bettie 98
  Martha 50
  Mary E. 59
  Nathaniel 69
  Nathaniel (Rev.) 83
  Nell 92
  S. G. 86
ODaniel, Cornelia 101
Oldham, Elizabeth 67,
  105

120

Stout (cont.)
Fadias 6
J. M. 68, 75, 77, 80,
82, 84, 85, 89, 93,
98, 104, 105
J. W. 85
John M. 74
Lucinda E. 106
Newton 70
Phebe 23
Ruth 7
Sarah M. 86
Straughan, Candas 37
E. H. 41, 45, 74, 79
E. K. 68
Eliza C. 73
Elizabeth 31, 39
F. M. 77
Julian 39
Margaret 64
Martha 11, 58
Mary 67
Presley 31
Sarah A. 76
Straughn, A. H. 52
A. M. 55
C. H. 86
E. C. 87
E. H. 45, 57, 58, 81,
83, 92
Elizab 83
Mary M. 104
Nancy J. 89
Street, Murdoc 84
Stroud, Caroline 95
Isaac H. 51
John S. 1, 69, 85
Lina 47
Martha E. S. 66
Mary J. 84
W. F. 79
Strudvaint, R. E. 84
Stuart, Alfred 80
Elenor 42
Elizabeth 33
Emely 78
Harriett 78
Mary A. 104
S. 6, 39
Solomon 30
Studivent, R. E. 59
Sturdivant, Harriet 19
K. E. 77
R. E. 65, 69, 71, 72,
77, 79, 82
Sulton, R. B. 79
Suther, Henry C. 39
Sutton, Robt (Rev.) 99,
100
Robt B. 77, 84, 102
Robt B. (Rev.) 87, 88,
94, 96
Swain, David L. 3
David L. (Gov.) 6, 36
Swayze, C. C. 69
Tally, Ann E. 97
B. 47, 51
Berry 44, 48, 49, 51,
58
C. C. 52, 54, 55, 70,
74, 90, 91
Green 107
Martha Jane 74
Misouria 49
Nancy 55, 63, 105
Nancy A. 55
Nicy 65
Parthenia A. 97

Tally (cont.)
Robt 55
Sarah 55
Sidney J. 92
Tenessee 78
W. M. 107
Wiley 52
Taylor, Apphia 36
J. T. 73
James P. 73
R. H. 60
W. A. 68
W. P. 34, 39, 53, 61,
63, 85, 95, 100
W. P. (Rev.) 39, 47,
48, 49, 52, 61, 73,
81
William 98
William P. (Rev.) 62
Wm. P. (Rev.) 58, 59,
61
Teag, Hezekiah 96
Teage, Rachel E. 58
Teague, Christopher 66
David N. 98
Edward 3
Edwin 66
Elizabeth Jane 39
Francis 95
Jacob 31
Margaret 58
Margarett M. 94
Maria 87
Moses R. 62
Peggy 18
Polly 23
Sally 11, 26
Samuel P. 68
Sarah Jane 63
Susanah 9
William 6
Temple, Ruth 24
Temples, Nancy 107
Polly 11
Tenny, John 104
Terry, Elizabeth 13
Thomas, Asa 99
Carlin 97
Delana 40
Delitha 103
Isabel 66
J. C. 63
J. H. 104
James 84
James C. 55
James M. 96
Joseph 16
Levina 101
M. C. 98
Mary J. 94
Mourning 40
Nany 59
Sallie Jane 85
Sally 55
Samuel 79
Sarah 21, 71
W. C. 97, 99
W. L. 97
William 36, 69
Thomason, Ann 93
Balaam 23
Gilly 36
Milley 23
Roberson 95
Thomlinson, Naby 106
Thompson, A. S. 100
Balaam W. S. 33
Catharine 105

Thompson (cont.)
Daniel 20
Edward 105
Eliza Ann 19
Elizabeth 19, 33
Elwood 50
George W. 8
John 33
Lindy 58
Louisa 45
Polly 11
Rachel 99
Sally 30
Samuel 59
Sarah 55
Thomas 3, 15, 26
William 12, 66
William (Jr.) 2
Thrailhill, M. 4
Thrailkill, Annie 107
Catharine 57
M. 41, 43, 52
Mary 101
Michael 41
Thrift, Charlotte 9
Emily 96
Isham 57
Martha 73
Peggy 34
Perry 34
Pinkney 83
Sam 43
Tilham, Young 73
Tillet, A. J. 86
J. (Rev.) 68
Tillett, John 71
S. 65
Tillman, Amie 55
Daniel 25
Eliza 90
Jane 52
Jeremiah 56
Polly 47
Tilman, A. J. 93
Aaron 20
Daniel 77
George 86
John 34
Tinen, J. W. (Rev.) 63,
76
John W. 58
Tiner, J. W. (Rev.) 75
John N. (Rev.) 73
Tinnen, J. W. (Rev.) 64
John W. (Rev.) 40
Tinnin, J. W. (Rev.) 38
Tinny, J. W. (Rev.) 64
Tolleson, Wm. 49
Tommolin, Patty 28
Toomer, A. D. 38
John J. 18
Trask, M. L. 84
Trice, Jane 98
Trip, Muied (?) 3
Tripp, Sarah 83
Wm 96
Tropling, James 3
True, Priscilla 76
Tucker, Fanny 24
Turlington, Randolph 65
Turner, A. N. (Rev.) 96
Arnal 68
Betteried (?) 37
Elizabeth 16
Sarah M. 103
Tyner, Emily C. 77
Jordan 77
Tyser, Mahala P. 59

124

Tyson, Frederick 36
  Jordan 38
Tysor, E. S. 41
  Elizabeth 6
  Emily 46
  Frances 4
  Jordan 40, 41, 46
  Joseph 41
  Josiah 49
  Maria 20
Underwood, Sally 29
  Solomon 35
Unthank, John 103
Upchurch, Bennet 61
  Henderson 66
  Isham 42
  James M. 66
  Jane 50
  Louvena 65
  Martha 37
  Mary A. 78
  Merritt 80
  Parthena 41
  Quinnetta 19, 42
  Rachael 53
  S. 61
  Simms 45
  Sims 9
  Wesley 90
Ussey, Martha 52
Utley, Emeline 65
  Jacob 38, 41
  Littlejohn 26
  Littlejohn (Rev.) 39
  Mary 40
Utly, Teretia 20
  Velania 71
Varrar, John 5
Vestal, A. 89
  Alfred 30
  Calvin 22
  Danl 55
  Elizabeth 50
  Henry Thomas 78
  Hiram 49
  Levena 58
  Mariah 60
  Mimy 21
  Peggey 30
  Polly 6
  Pyrena E. 38
  Rebecca 87
  Sally 23
  Susanna 8
  Zimri 23
Vick, Lucy Ann 55
Vinson, George W. 90
Waddell, James 59
  Robert W. 81
  Thomas 77
Waddill, Anne 34
  Margaret (Mrs.) 34
  Thomas 34
  Thos 34
Walace, Jane 103
Walden, Elizabeth 1
  John 100
  Susan 48
Walker, Catharine B. 38
  Eliza 11
  Margaret J. 35
  Margarett 43
  Nancy 60
  William 35
Walls, A. J. 46
  Harrison 85
Wamack, Rebecca 4
Ward, B. R. 64

Ward (cont.)
  Henry 37
  James 57
  James M. 91
  Julia C. 5
  Kesiah 6
  Martha 104
  Thos 106
  Wm 47, 54
Warren, Sarah 34
  Susanah 4
Wates, J. T. 92
Watkins, Daniel S. 106
Watson, Calvin 46
  Elisha 44
  Eliza 49
  Emma E. 44
  J. W. 78
  James E. 102
  James G. 76
  Jane 11
  Mary J. 8
  Mathew D. 89
Watters, Henry Jackson
    43
Way, Alexander 89
  Benjamin 25
  James D. 61
  John 33, 48
  Stanford 42
  William 33
Weaver, Arthur 15
Webb, R. S. 89
Weber, Henne 43
Webster, A. M. 102
  Alvis 102
  Basel E. 76
  Ben 50
  Eli W. 7
  Fuller 92
  Haratt 68
  Isaiah M. 47
  James 35
  Martha J. 96
  Mary A. 86
  Peggy 7
  R. 43, 47, 56, 57, 60,
    85
  Richard 31, 39, 42,
    44, 62, 71, 72, 76,
    93
  Richard B. 71
  Robert 85
  Sarah 6
  Simon F. 35
  W. S. 90
Welch, Edmond 35
  Eli 60
  Emily 41
  James 36, 63
  Martha 47
  Oran 53
  Rebecca J. 105
Wellons, J. W. 73, 76
Wells, Benjamin 2
  Charity 34
  Eliza 39
  Hannah 14
  Hiram 105
Welsh, Benj 103
West, M. E. (Mrs.) 97
  Nancy 40
Wh---, Jas. W. 70
Wheeler, Eliza 77
  J. W. 73
Which, Cargle 97
Whit, Carizan 57
Whitaker, Fanny 61

Whitaker (cont.)
  Nelly 6
White, A. M. 54
  Drucilla 2
  Eliza 83
  F. J. 46
  Jno. M. 45
  John 55, 69
  Joseph J. 71
  Lucinda 33
  Mary 104
  Mary A. 68
  Newton 71
  Priscilla 43
  Simon 43
  Tabitha 56
  Thos B. 75
  William 43
Whitehead, Arthur 93
  Elizabeth 1
  James 35
  John 35, 56
  Josiah 29
  Lewis 106
  Matilda 105
  Richard 93
  Sarah E. 91
  Thomas 2
  William 1
Whitfield, Canatha L. 47
Wicker, Archibald 101
  Benjamin 9
  Caswell D. 40
  Catharine 3
  Cathrine 77
  Elizabeth 9, 18, 20,
    79
  Harriet 98
  John D. 103
  Prudence 45
  Wm. M. 74
Wilcox, G. W. 94
Wilken, George W. 49
Wilkerson, Zebulon 35
Wilkey, John 101
Wilkie, Ann 107
  Elizabeth M. 60
  Mary 42
  William 36
Wilkinson, Rachal 16
Wilkison, James 10
Willen, L. K. 72
Willet, Darke 91
  Ecameliza 32
  Elizabeth 84
  Jane 54
  Joshua 32
  Mary J. 100
  Phebe 32
  Sarah 101
  Thos C. 54
Willett, Charles 43
  Phebe 36
Williams, A. T. 58
  Adaline 97
  Andrew G. 43
  Apphia 6
  Benjamin 26
  C. C. 85, 92
  Camelia 100
  Caroline 80
  Catharine 2
  David 86
  David P. 34
  Dealan 66
  Delia 34
  Della A. 102
  E. A. 106

125

Williams (cont.)
  Elenor 8
  Eliza 14
  Enoch 25, 90
  Ester Ann 90
  Francis 97
  George 14
  H. 88
  Hannah 28
  Harbard 41
  J. 39, 64
  James A. P. 67
  James M. 98
  John 48, 57
  John A. 106
  Levi B. 74
  Louisa 72
  Lovy 3
  Lydia 60
  Mariah 31
  Mary A. 40
  Murphy 56
  Nathan S. 36
  Nicy 38
  Noel 36
  Rebecca J. 72
  Sally 7, 8
  Sarah 90
  Talitha 45
  William 64, 86
Williamson, David 70
  Susan 95
  Thomas F. 61
  Virginia 86
Willins, J. W. (Rev.) 64
Willis, R. A. (Rev.) 94
Willon, J. W. 73
Willons, J. W. 73
Wilson, A. T. 47
  Andrew 52
  Beedy 14
  Candas 10
  Hammett 50
  Henry 14
  Isley A. 70
  J. C. 16, 42, 57, 63,
    84
  J. C. (Rev.) 47, 48,
    57
  J. O. 72
  John 25
  Nancy 4, 43
  Robert 94
  Sarah 15
  Troy 19
  W. C. 98, 106
  William 32
  Willis C. 101
Winbley, Lucy 9
Windham, Elbert 85
  Martha 16
Wise, Jane 7
Witherspoon, Sidney 63
Woble, Lidia 82
Womack, Green 21
  Jefferson 58
  Lucy A. 73
  Martha 60
  Mary 40
  Nelly 4
  Sarah J. 62
Womble, Amanda J. 35
  Elisha 45
  Eliza Ann 45
  George W. 60
  Henry L. 62
  J. W. 103
  Jesse 5, 20

Womble (cont.)
  John M. 49
  John T. 58
  Joseph 41
  Marcus 69
  Margarett L. 94
  Martha A. 50
  Mary 72, 89
  Milly 34
  Nancy 65
  Nancy Jane 56
  Ruth C. 47
  Thomas 12
  W. 49
  William 103
Wood, Polly 34
Woodall, Lucinda 7
Woodell, B. H. 101
Woods, Gillico 27
Woody, Nancy 69
Workman, Martha 19
  Riffin 69
  Sally 40
Worth, D. (Rev.) 61
  Daniel (Rev.) 60, 61
Wortham, William 72
Wren, M. H. 102
Wrenn, John 43
Wright, Della 95
  Elizabeth 63
  Frances 71
  Hiram 21
  Isabella 58
  James 29
  Julia 45
  L. J. 96
  Nancy 70
  Sarah 29
Wynn, Caroline 72
Wysor, Julia 58
Yaes, Lucian B. 41
Yarbor, A. M. 44
Yarboro, A. M. 45, 48
  Frederick 48
Yarborough, Emeline
    Esperann Florentine
    41
  Isabella 49
  S. 88
Yarbro, J. S. 67
  Thos 72
Yarbrough, A. M. 58, 60,
    66, 67, 69, 71, 74,
    82, 83
  Elizabeth 69
  Emeline Ester Ann
    Florentine 25
  M. 82
  Malinda 76
  Wm. 66
  Y. S. 66
Yates, A. W. 59
  Ann E. 47
  V. A. T. 61
Yeargin, Hillery H. 2
Ylarbrough, A. M. 81
York, B. 54
  Louisa A. 66
  W. F. 50
Yorke, Elizabeth M. 97
Young, Allen 40
  Lucy 66
Younger, Rebecca 31
Zachary, William 81
  Wm. 66
Zachry, Jonathan 59
Zackary, Wm. 65
Zackery, Johnathan 50